Cue Tips

based on the teachings of
Chris Raftis

For further information
contact

C. R. Billiards
P. O. Box 02903
Detroit, MI.
48202, USA.

Cue Tips-new and expanded edition
c1989 Chris Raftis

Original drawings and design:
Chris Raftis
Sketches from photos by:
Jagruti Kadakia
Technical assistance by:
Nick Raftis

Printed in USA

Published in Detroit,MI., USA

ISBN   0-9625197-9-0

Dedicated to those individuals who
desire to do more than just bang
the balls around the table

and to Miss Lanhua Wei Wang who was
the inspiration for starting this
creative writing

and to Mister Rick McCallum who
suggested the production of this
book.

The author: Chris Raftis

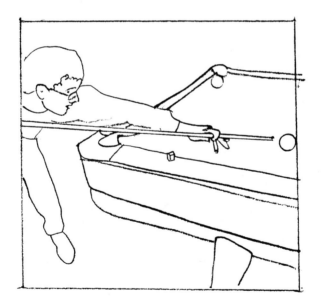

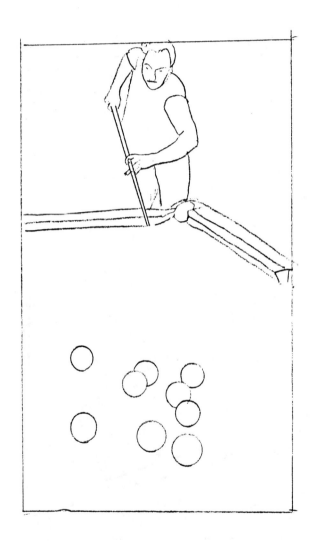

Contents

Introduction to pocket billiards   1

Instructions:
    Styles of play   5
    Ball speeds   6
    Terminology   7
    Helpful hints   17

Shotmaking:
    Cut shots   23
    Bank shots   26
    Straight in shots   28
    Draw shots   29
    Kick shots   30
    Jump and umbrella   31
    Practice shots   31

Games:
    Nine ball   133
    Eight ball   144
    Eight ball with nine balls   150
    Six ball with a special   150
        five ball
Position play   153

Competing   155

Mechanical devices   163

Authors' history   177

Introduction to pocket billiards

Why do people play pocket billiards? Pocket billiards is a very demanding activity. The game requires the following skills and abilities: concentration, patience, accumulation of knowledge and physical dexterity.

In playing pocket billiards you have to "read the table", which means that you have to know what the sequence of shots are that are necessary to win the game. In order to accomplish this activity you need to have some prior knowledge of how to make the shots or someone who recognizes your abilities has to tell you the shot sequence.

In order to read the table you will first have to practice the twenty four cut shots, the sixteen bank shots and the ball speed chart. Initial practice requires the use of one ball and advanced practice would require the use of two balls, in other words the cue ball and a desired object ball.

While playing pocket billiards by yourself, you can compete by acknowledging how many times in succession you are able to score a certain shot or shot sequence.

When competing with an opponent, you may compete on a social basis or on a serious basis.

Many of the advanced players began instruction in their youth. By starting young a player can develop into an accomplished player by adult age.

Pocket billiards is a wonderful activity for women and children. The balls weigh about five and one half ounces and a cue stick would weigh between fourteen and twenty one ounces. When the cue stick is held slightly behind the balance point then the weight of the cue is only felt slightly. The controlled movement of the cue determines the force or speed imparted to the cue ball and then subsequently to the object ball.

Pocket billiards is a great mind occupier. When a person becomes

attracted to playing pocket
billiards then he can play for
hours on end.

I wish you every success in playing
pocket billiards. May all the
desired object balls roll into the
pockets and may you win all your
matches.

Don't forget that the world of
knowledge flows through books. So
you have this book, now you must
take advantage and learn all that
is to be learned from this book.
All the essential information
regarding pocket billiards is
explained in this book especially
as relates to practical billiard
mathematics.

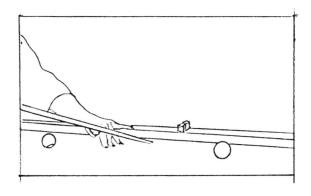

Instructions

Styles of play

The recommended style of play is called "rifling", which means that you place your eye over the center line of the cue and aim the cue just as you would a rifle. In other words you look down the cue as if it were a rifle barrel. Also the body is bent forward from the hips so that the eye is near the cue stick. If you are left handed you sight with your right eye and if you are right handed you sight with your left eye. See examples of rifling in photos illustrations.

Another interesting technique used with "rifling" is called "cocking the cue". Cocking the cue means that after you groove the shot by performing a few warm up strokes, you pull the cue back to the farthest position, hold it temporarily and then press the cue forward.

Ball speeds

The ball speeds are predetermined as one through ten. Speeds one and two are called "very soft"; three and four are "soft"; five and six are "medium"; seven and eight are "hard"; and nine and ten are "very hard". These speed designations are arbitrary and are for the purposes of instruction. See diagram.

In order to practice the ball speeds it is necessary that the cue stick be held level and that the cue tip strike the cue ball through the center of the ball.

To begin the practice of ball speeds, place a ball, preferably the cue ball, near the rail. Now strike the ball so that it travels half the distance of the table. This is speed number one. Replace the ball near the rail and strike it so that it travels one length of the table to the rail. This is speed number two. Replace the ball near the rail and strike it so that it travels one and one half the length of the table for speed number three. Continue this procedure following the diagram until you reach speed number ten.

While performing this exercise, strike through the center of the ball so that when the ball rebounds it does not deviate from a straight line. This is called "cue ball control" and even professionals perform this practice.

Terminology

There are many words and phrases used in this book that need explanation. Also pocket billiard play necessitates a certain language that should be learned.

The following is an alphabetical list of those words or phrases with their explanation:

Angle of incidence: The angle formed when a ball strikes the cushion from the balls' starting point.

Angle of reflection: The opposite angle to the angle of incidence when the ball strikes the cushion without spin or influence. The angle of reflection is equal to the angle of incidence when the ball striking the cushion turns over after being struck in dead center.

Apex ball: The front ball in the rack

Ball bangers: Players who are not serious about playing and who play for social reasons and to relieve tension.

Bank shot: Rebounding a ball from one or more cushions.

Billiards: Striking a sphere with a tapered instrument and playing on a table without pockets. Pocket billiards then is a game where balls are struck with a cue and pocketed on a billiards table that has pockets.

Billiard hall: A room where billiard tables are maintained for play by the public.

Billiard Lounge: A billiard hall that has been decorated with decorator lights, carpeting and a snack bar. Billiard lounges cater to women, children and families whereas a billiard hall is normally frequented by men only.

Black ball: The black ball is also known as the eight ball.

Body force: Body force is normally confined to the break shot.

Break shot: Striking the racked balls with the cue ball.

Cocked cue stick: The cue is held temporarily on the back swing for a final assessment of the shot at hand.

Consecutive order: Following a numerical sequence or a pre-planned sequence numbered mentally by the player.

Cue ball in hand: Your opponent has fouled therefore you are allowed to place the cue ball on the table to your best advantage. This is permitted in nine ball on any shot after the break shot.

Dead ball: When the cue ball is struck in the center with a level cue and the cue ball scoots across the cloth before striking an object ball or cushion then this is a dead ball.

On full impact with an object ball the cue ball will stop "dead" at the point of impact.

Degree of adjustment: When the desired object ball and the cue ball are in a line with a desired pocket then the degree of deviation between the object ball and the pocket is equal to the degree of adjustment for aligning the cue stick with the cue ball.

Degree of deviation: The angle formed when a line is drawn between the object ball and the center of a favorable pocket with a connecting line drawn from the center of the object ball to the area of deviation from the center of the pocket. This statement is only true when the desired object ball and the cue ball are in a line with a desired pocket.

English: When a ball deviates from a straight path after being struck that ball is said to be under the influence of english. Also by striking the cue ball off the perpendicular center, english or spin is applied.

Favored position: The position on the table where you place the cue ball after you opponent has fouled in nine ball.

Foul: A foul is something that happens out of the ordinary or something that should not have happened. Examples are: jumping the cue ball or an object ball off the table; pocketing the cue ball; moving a ball accidentally with the body; striking the wrong ball in consecutive order; not striking the desired object ball; and not driving a ball to a rail after contact.

Freeze out: Betting all the monies on one set match of games.

Front runner: A player who is able to win a few fast games and then remain unchallenged is a front runner.

Full strength shot: By moving the cue quickly and with the aid of body movement you are able to produce a full strength shot for striking the racked balls.

Handicapping: To give your opponent a head start, lead or spot or to minimize your playing abilities is called handicapping and is necessary if you are the better player.

Hard: A designated speed of the ball or a difficult shot.

Hustling: To take advantage of your opponent by not revealing your true strength as a player.

Jacked up: To play with the cue stick held in the air. This is a form of handicapping.

Kick shot: To strike a cushion prior to striking a desired object ball is called a kick shot.

Lag: Rolling a ball to the end of the table and back to the starting position or the rail is called a lag.

Lock up: A player is said to be "locked up" when he has virtually no chance to win.

Making a plan: To make a plan on how to run out a sequence of balls after reading the table.

Milking the game: Winning a percentage of games in order not to be recognized as the better player.

Multiple bank angles: To strike two or more cushions with a ball.

Numbered balls: Plastic or ceramic balls with a number imprinted on the face. In pocket billiards the balls are numbered one through fifteen.

Object ball angle: The object ball angle is determined by the location of a desired pocket.

Obstructing ball: A ball that is in a line between a desired object ball and a favored pocket or between the cue ball and a desired object ball. Also a ball obstructing the path for a desired hit point on a cushion.

Offending player: A player who has committed a foul.

Out of stroke: A player who has lost the technique of striking the cue ball with the cue stick is said to be out of stroke.

Paralleling: To draw a mental line between the object ball and the cue ball and then aligning the cue stick parallel to that line in order to complete the shot pattern. Also to draw a mental line between a ball and a cushion between two known bank angle lines.

Percentage: Used to determine your ability at cut and bank shots. Knowing your percentage is helpful when reading the table to determine the shot sequence.

Playing out: Pocketing the last balls on the table which is also known as "running out".

Pocketing: To cause a ball to enter a pocket.

Principal ball: The last ball prior to pocketing the game ball. This is the ball that is used for playing position for the final shot.

Rack: Rack refers to two things. First a rack is an instrument used for racking the balls. Second a rack is a grouping of balls positioned on the table for the start of a game.

Reading the table: To examine the position of the balls and then make a mental shot sequence plan.

Rifle sighting: Sighting down the cue stick similar to sighting down a rifle.

Rotation order: The balls in consecutive number sequence.

Run out: To pocket all the remaining balls in one shot sequence.

Safety: A difficult leave of the balls.

Scratch: Means that the cue ball has entered a pocket.

Selected pocket: A desired pocket or designated pocket.

Shot pattern: A players preference for a certain shot or a predesignated shot.

Shot sequence: A selected grouping of shots preferred by a player.

Snooker: To hide the cue ball from a direct path to the desired object ball.

Spot: First spot means to advance an opponents' score and second a spot is a round disc glued on the table and used for spotting a ball after a foul stroke.

Stroking arm: For a right handed player it is the right arm and for a left handed player it is the left arm.

Throw: To influence a ball to travel in other than a straight line.

Helpful advices

A. Study long and you study wrong. When you first approach the table and read the table, you will make decisions. After making these decisions, you have to be determined not to change your mind. First you visualize making the shots and then you execute your plan. Don't make plans and then keep changing them.

B. Different strokes for different folks. No one player plays exactly like another. It can be explained to you why you should play a shot in a certain way and it can be explained why one method may be better than another but ultimately it is up to you to determine your style of play.

C. Wipe or brush the chalk onto the cue tip. Place the chalk on the cue tip as an abrasive for contact with the cue ball. It is not necessary to chalk the cue tip for every shot but it is recommended to chalk the cut tip often. By grinding the chalk into the cue tip you may remove more chalk than you

put on which defeats the purpose of
the chalk.

D. If you think that you should
play a safety then play a safety.
You have to be decisive even if
your decision is wrong. When it's
your turn at the table and you read
the table and decide that the best
shot is a safety then play the best
safety that you can play.

E. Miss the shot on the
professional side of the pocket.
You should play a shot pattern for
the proper entrance to the pocket.
For long angle shots into the
corner pocket you have to
especially avoid hitting the long
rail prior to the pocket opening.
For short angle shots you have to
avoid hitting the near corner.

F. How do you make a thin hit on
the object ball. Line up the edge
of the object ball with the edge of
the cue ball by paralleling your
line of aim. You have to draw an
imaginary line between the edge of
the cue ball and the edge of the
object ball and then you have to
parallel that line with the cue

stick. There should be a small
"click" sound when the cue ball
meets the object ball. In other
words the cue ball must
reconstitute itself after impacting
the object ball. This requires a
greater speed on the cue ball in
order to generate a slow speed on
the object ball.

G. How do you make a half ball
hit. Align the cue through the
center of the cue ball to the
outside edge of the object ball and
then strike the cue ball.

H. Here is a special procedure to
use when the cue ball and the
object ball are both in a line with
a desired pocket. Aim the cue
stick through the center of the cue
ball and in line with the center of
the pocket. By aiming at a point
in the pocket the object ball will
automatically enter the pocket. It
is easier to aim the cue ball for
the pocket opening than it is to
try to pick a spot on the object
ball to strike or to aim to cover
the object ball with the cue ball.
Another procedure is when the
object ball is slightly out of line

with the cue ball and the desired
pocket then it is only necessary to
adjust the alignment of the cue
stick for the amount or degree of
deviation of alignment. Further
explanation is given by diagram.

I. A procedure for playing
position when the object ball is
near a desired pocket opening. You
may cut the object ball into one
side of the pocket or the other
which would be determined by the
position of the second desired
object ball on the table. The
pocket opening is two balls width
which allows for leeway when
playing the shot for position.
Take advantage of this easy
opportunity to play position by not
shooting the shot straight into the
pocket.

J. Always trust your first
judgement. Your mind can be your
worst enemy or your best friend.
Train your mind by reading the
table and knowing your ability to
score, then this information will
come forward when you analyze the
shot patterns. Trust your
experience and judgement.

K. Always acknowledge a good scoring opportunity. Sometimes the object ball is on a line from the center of the pocket and the pocket opening which means that you have the maximum scoring opportunity. When you have a wide angle entry into the pocket then your scoring opportunity is better than a narrow angle.

L. Profit by your opponents' mistakes. This is the difference between winning and losing. If two players are of equal strengths then the player who doesn't make mistakes or who profits by his opponents' mistakes will win the game.

M. Make the shot clean. In other words do not touch the rail edge in front of the pocket or the corner of the pocket which then causes the ball to wobble before dropping into the pocket. This requires a little more analysis and concentration to accomplish.

N. The deeper the ball indents the cushion the smaller the degree of angle of rebound.

O. Once the cue ball is struck you cannot change its path by contortions or wishing. Once you strike the cue ball the shot pattern is finished. You have to do everything prior to striking the cue ball. If you have properly executed the shot then nothing will stop you from scoring.

P. Play half safeties if you do not think you can score. If you have been getting a low percentage on the shot pattern or if your opponent has left you a difficult shot then play a safety. If your percentages are not too bad and the shot is not too difficult you may want to play a half-safety. In other words you try to score but you adjust the speed of the ball so in case you miss your opponent will not be left with a set up.

Q. Practice makes perfect if you practice the right concepts. First you must accept good instruction then you practice accomplishing that instruction.

Shotmaking

A. Cut Shots

There are twenty four cut shots illustrated in this book. The drawings are full size and can be used in place of templates. There are two ways that the drawing may be used, as follows:

First you may photocopy them and cut them out. Then place one on the table for practice exercises. When placing the drawing on the table you will need to point the arrow accurately at the desired portion of the pocket opening or the desired hit point on the rail. Punch a hole in the center of the object ball circle or place a ring binder reinforcement inside the seventeen thirty second circle to help locate the object ball properly in the center of the object ball circle. Align the cue stick through the center of the cue ball and in line with the center of the phantom cue ball shown in the drawing. Strike the cue ball through the center keeping the alignment with the center of the

23

phantom cue ball. If you perform
this instruction properly then the
object ball should enter the pocket
opening. Reposition the drawing in
several locations about the table
and continue the same execution.
It may be of some help to place a
piece of chalk on the rail in
alignment with the cue ball, the
phantom cue ball and the sighting
point on the diagram. When you are
proficient with one drawing change
to another. Continue this
procedure until you are expert with
all the twenty four shot patterns.
See figure twenty four.

The same pattern of twenty four
shots identified arbitrarily in
degrees of cut from ninety to two
hundred and seventy can also be
identified as from zero to ninety
degrees right and zero to ninety
degrees left.

Another way to utilize the drawings
is to photocopy them; then cut out
the shot patterns; then cut out the
three inner circles. Place the
diagram in position on the table.
Then place one half inch removable
paper dots inside the small circle

openings. Now remove the template
from the table. Align the cue stick
with the center of the cue ball,
the phantom cue ball dot and the
sighting point dot. You previously
placed the object ball on the
object ball dot. Now strike the cue
ball keeping the alignment with the
two dots. The object ball should
enter the pocket opening if you
have performed the instruction
correctly.

Another system of cut shots is to
extend a line from the desired
portion of the pocket opening
through the center of the object
ball and for a short distance
beyond. Draw another imaginary line
from the center of the phantom cue
ball to the center of the cue ball.
This then is the back angle cut
from zero to ninety degrees right
and left.

An additional series of cut shots
are performed when the object ball
is in a position to obstruct a
center line drawn from the center
of the cue ball to the desired
pocket opening. When this situation
is available then you place a

25

phantom object ball in the desired portion of the pocket opening. Now draw a line from the center of the cue ball to the center of the phantom object ball. Now draw a line from the center of the object ball to the center of the phantom object ball. Next draw a line from the center of the cue ball through the center of the object ball until the line touches a rail or pocket opening. Erase the portion of the line between the cue ball and the object ball. Now the angle formed by the two lines extending from the center of the object ball is called the angle of deviation; therefore if we apply this same degree of angle from the cue ball center then we have the degree of adjustment necessary to make the shot. Now strike the cue ball along the line of adjustment and make the cut shot. It is not too difficult once you understand the principles. See figure.

B. Bank shots

One, two, three, four and five rail shots will be illustrated. In the one and two rail shots, the angle of incidence equals the angle of reflection. See figures.

In the three and four rail banks this is not exactly true due to the impact of the ball on the cushion at a greater angle.

The contact point of the rail with the ball is approximately one half inch above the ball center. In addition the wider the degree of angle upon impact, the greater the amount of slide which will cause a deviation in the ball path due to the influence of imparted spin. See figure.

Three bank shots are illustrated.

When the reference angle is known, then a bank shot can be computed by interpretation. See figures.

Another system illustrating the angle of incidence equals the angle of reflection is shown in figures, entitled "playing through the diamonds". In these illustrations it is necessary that the line of the cue stick travel over the rail marking. Also the speed of the ball

should be such that the ball upon
contact with the cushion "turns
over" and should not slide or
scoot.

When banking a ball with a force
harder than necessary, the ball
will rebound at a smaller degree of
angle. The opposite is true when
banking a ball with a force less
than necessary, the ball will tend
to float or return at a wider
degree of angle.

One way of making sure that you are
striking accurately is to place a
piece of chalk on the rail edge at
the point of contact. If the ball
is struck accurately then the chalk
will jump off the table.

Another method is to use the angle
of refraction or the back angle to
determine the beginning angle.

C. Straight in shots

You must make sure that the cue
ball is struck in the center or
below the center when executing
straight in shots in order to avoid

the cue ball following the object ball into the pocket.

One system of alignment is to align the cue through the cue ball to a point beyond the pocket opening. This instruction may help you to pocket a greater percentage of balls.

Another system of aiming is ball cover. If the shot is straight in, then when the cue ball fully covers the face of the object ball the shot is assured.

Another method of sighting is to select a point in the pocket opening that will ensure success when the object ball is struck.

D. Draw shots

The draw shot is executed by playing the cue tip through the cue ball to an imaginary point on the cloth. The important thing to remember here is to follow through until the cue tip actually touches the cloth. If this is not possible due to the position of the balls then the follow through should be

as complete as practical with a
quickness of wrist movement to
facilitate the shot.

The closeness of the point on the
cloth to the cue ball will
determine the depth of the draw
action. The further away the point
the longer the draw. See
illustrations.

E. Kick shots

One detailed illustration
consisting of four drawings is
shown in figures.

Two illustrations of kick shots
using the extended table theory are
shown in figures. In these
illustrations the instruction is
that an extended equal distance
creates an equal angle.

Other kick shots for practice
purposes are shown in figures.

F. Jump and umbrella shots

The jump shot is illustrated with sketches.

The "umbrella" shot is illustrated. The cue ball after contact with the first object ball and the rail opens up like an umbrella or in other words leaves the rail at a greater angle than that which it entered.

G. Practice Shots

Practice accurate striking by placing a piece of chalk on the rail. If you strike the rail accurately the chalk will jump off the table.

Using the cut shot templates, move them into various positions on the table and by accurate striking you will receive a well-rounded perspective of the different cut shot patterns.

Roll a ball up and down the center line of the table and observe if the ball deviates from the center line. Continue practicing until the ball does not deviate. This

practice will give you confidence
that you are striking the ball in a
proper manner and that your line up
and aim are also proper.

Place two balls in your hand. Roll
one ball toward the farthest corner
pocket at a moderate speed. Now
quickly place the other ball on the
table and strike the ball in such a
manner as to reach the first ball
and pocket it in the corner pocket.
In order to get a good percentage
try to have the balls meet about
three quarters distance on the
table. Rolling the first ball at a
good speed is paramount to success.

Practice banking with one ball
using the bank angles shown in the
diagrams. When you gain some
proficiency start using two balls
by striking the second ball with
the first ball. Use a center ball
hit in the beginning and sufficient
speed for the object ball to travel
past the pocket opening. Continue
this practice by varying the angles
of entry into the rail.

Practice "reading the table" by
placing balls on the table in

random order and then try to pocket all the balls in succession by always playing position for the second shot.

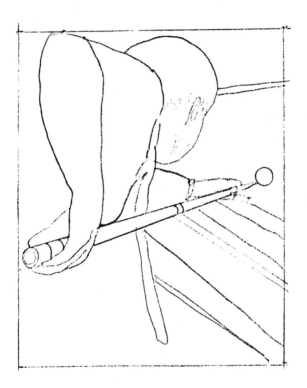

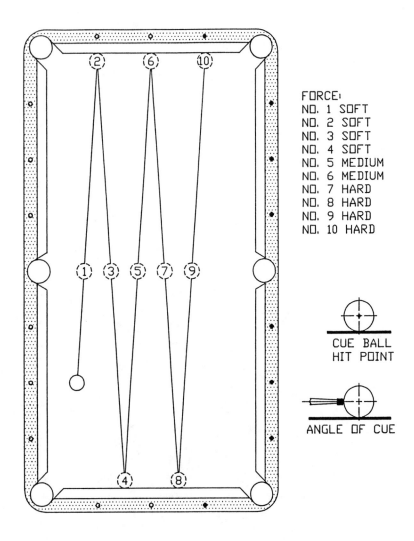

FORCE:
NO. 1 SOFT
NO. 2 SOFT
NO. 3 SOFT
NO. 4 SOFT
NO. 5 MEDIUM
NO. 6 MEDIUM
NO. 7 HARD
NO. 8 HARD
NO. 9 HARD
NO. 10 HARD

CUE BALL
HIT POINT

ANGLE OF CUE

-A NORMAL BALL SPEED CHART

34

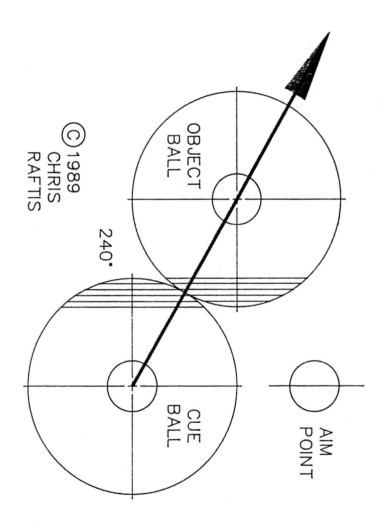

OBJECT
BALL

© 1989
CHRIS
RAFTIS

240°

CUE
BALL

AIM
POINT

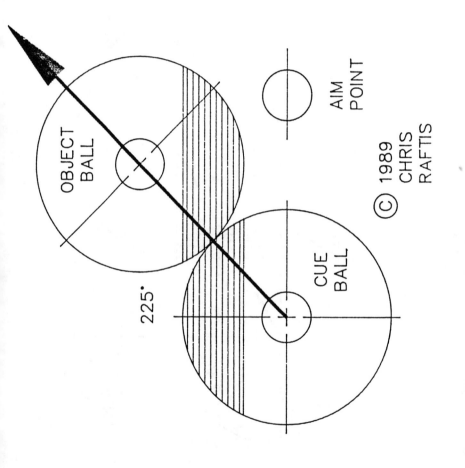

OBJECT BALL

225°

CUE BALL

AIM POINT

© 1989 CHRIS RAFTIS

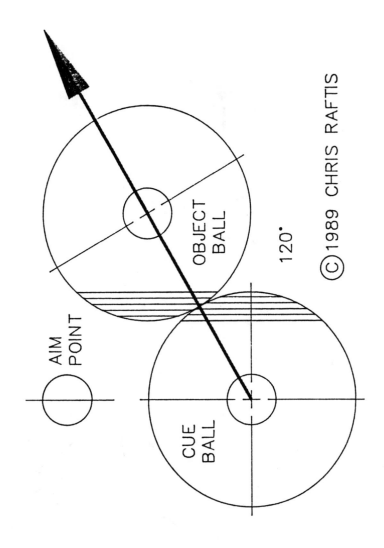

AIM
POINT

CUE
BALL

OBJECT
BALL

120°

©1989 CHRIS RAFTIS

37

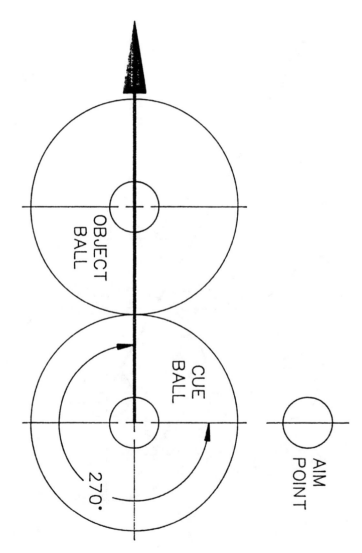

OBJECT
BALL

CUE
BALL

270°

AIM
POINT

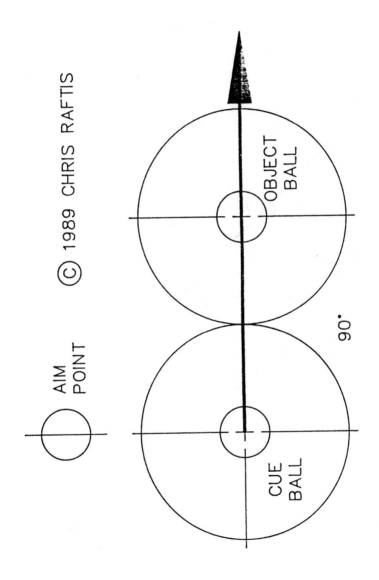

AIM
POINT

© 1989 CHRIS RAFTIS

OBJECT
BALL

CUE
BALL

90°

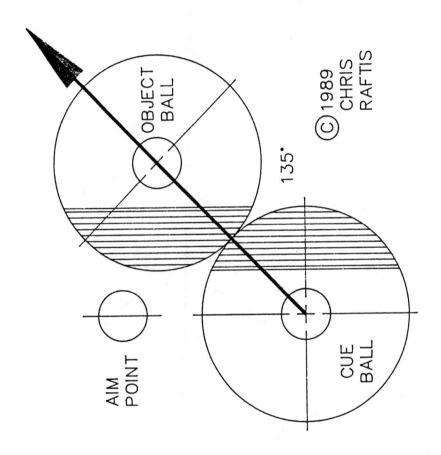

OBJECT
BALL

135°

© 1989 CHRIS
RAFTIS

AIM
POINT

CUE
BALL

40

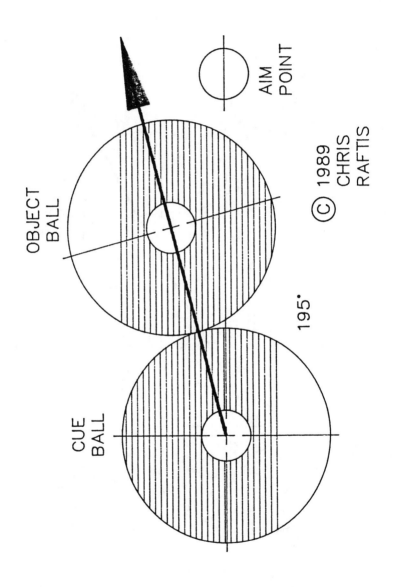

OBJECT
BALL

CUE
BALL

AIM
POINT

© 1989
CHRIS
RAFTIS

195°

41

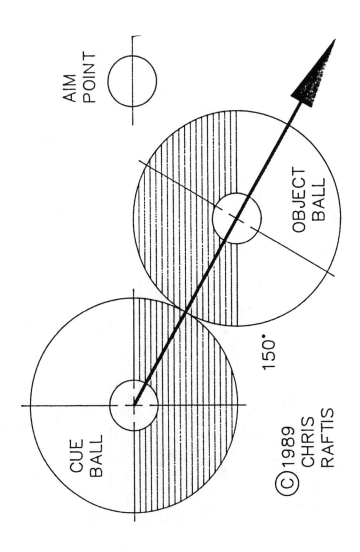

AIM POINT

OBJECT BALL

CUE BALL

150°

© 1989 CHRIS RAFTIS

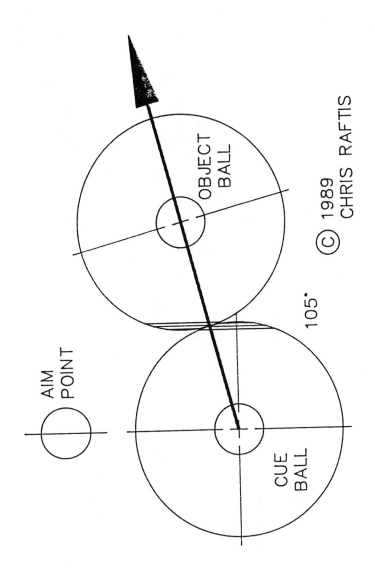

AIM
POINT

OBJECT
BALL

CUE
BALL

105°

© 1989
CHRIS RAFTIS

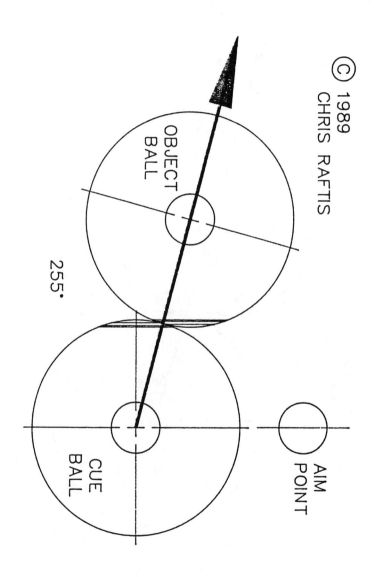

© 1989
CHRIS RAFTIS

OBJECT
BALL

255°

CUE
BALL

AIM
POINT

44

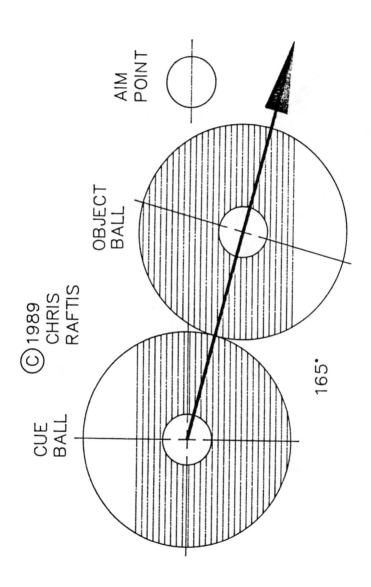

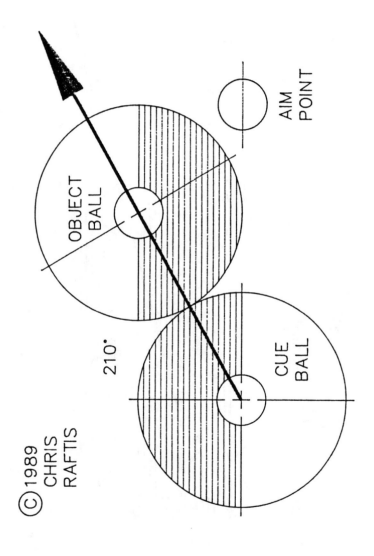

AIM POINT

OBJECT BALL

210°

CUE BALL

© 1989 CHRIS RAFTIS

46

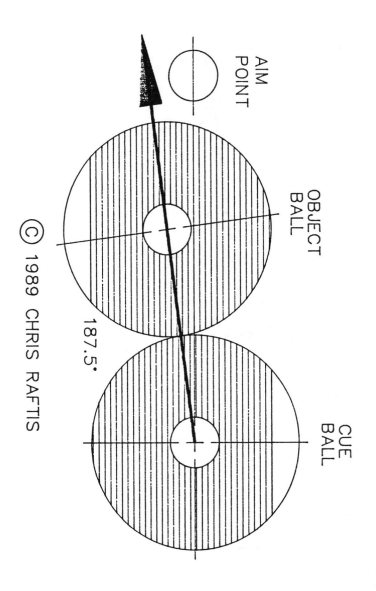

AIM
POINT

OBJECT
BALL

CUE
BALL

187.5°

© 1989 CHRIS RAFTIS

47

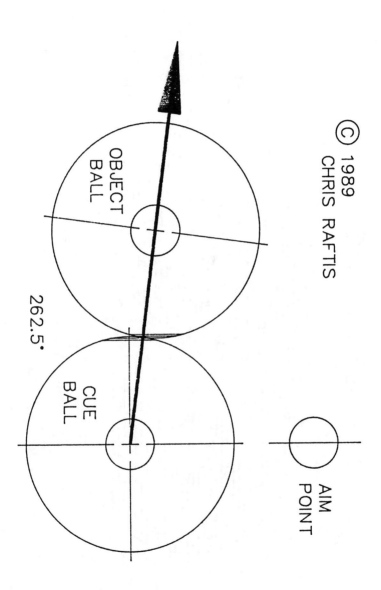

262.5°

OBJECT
BALL

CUE
BALL

AIM
POINT

© 1989
CHRIS RAFTIS

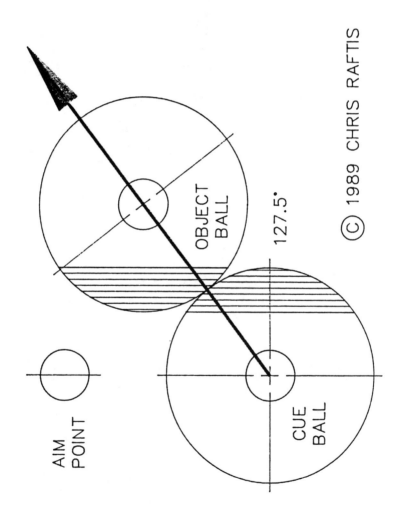

AIM
POINT

OBJECT
BALL

CUE
BALL

127.5°

© 1989 CHRIS RAFTIS

49

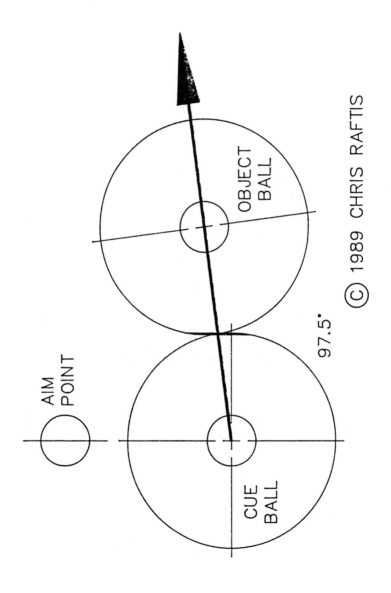

AIM
POINT

OBJECT
BALL

CUE
BALL

97.5°

© 1989 CHRIS RAFTIS

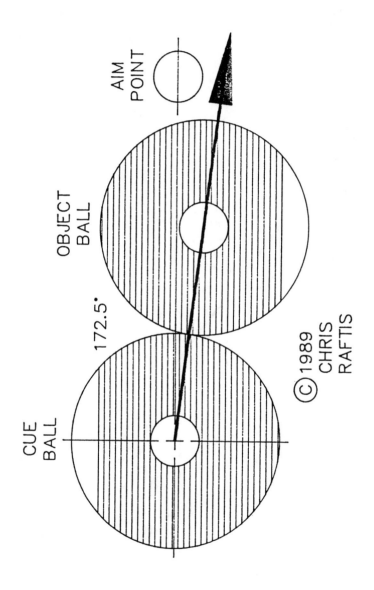

AIM
POINT

OBJECT
BALL

172.5°

CUE
BALL

© 1989
CHRIS
RAFTIS

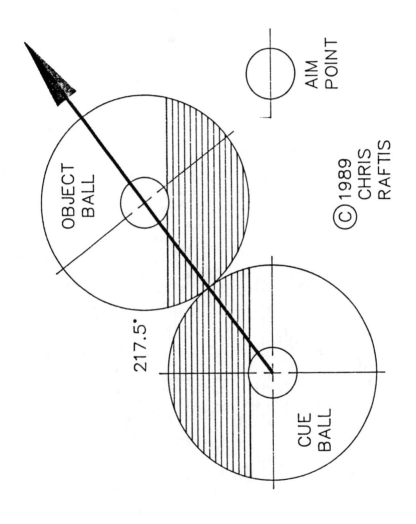

AIM
POINT

© 1989
CHRIS
RAFTIS

OBJECT
BALL

217.5°

CUE
BALL

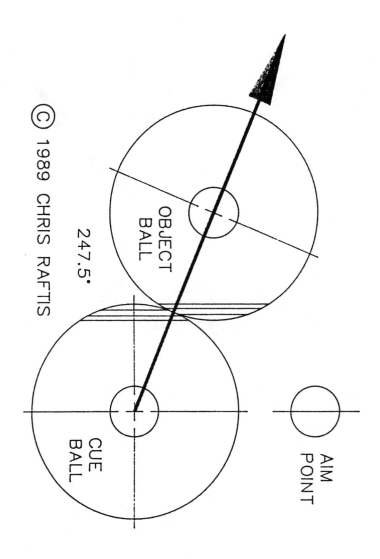

OBJECT BALL

CUE BALL

AIM POINT

247.5°

© 1989 CHRIS RAFTIS

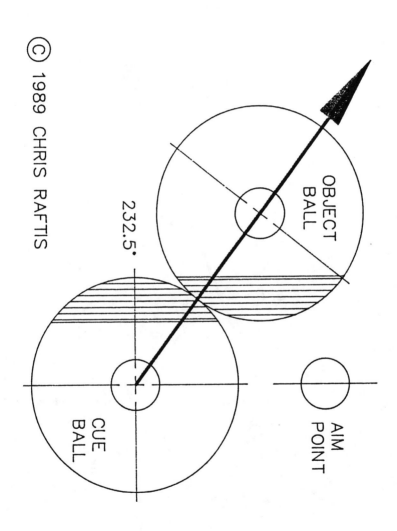

© 1989 CHRIS RAFTIS

232.5°

OBJECT
BALL

CUE
BALL

AIM
POINT

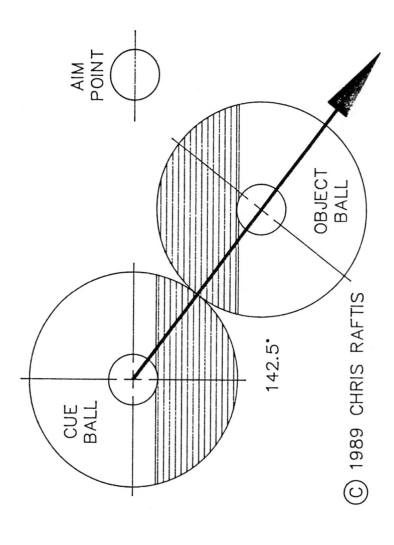

AIM
POINT

OBJECT
BALL

142.5°

CUE
BALL

Ⓒ 1989 CHRIS RAFTIS

55

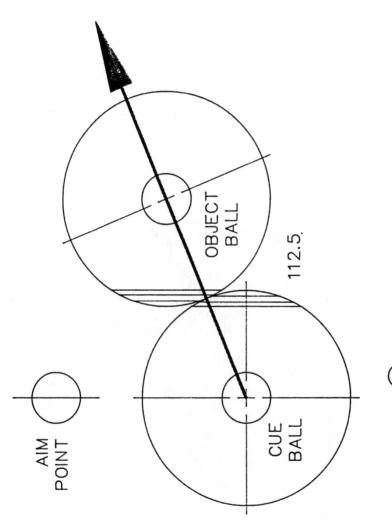

AIM
POINT

OBJECT
BALL

112.5.

CUE
BALL

© 1989 CHRIS RAFTIS

56

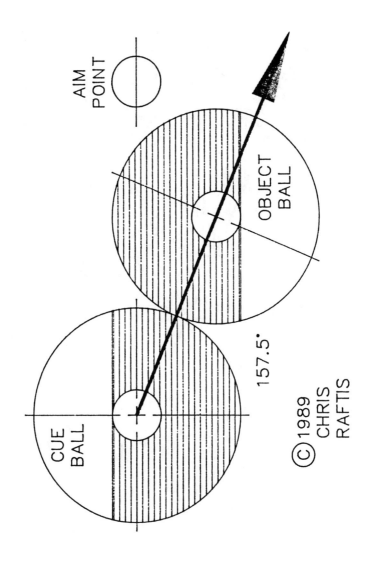

AIM
POINT

OBJECT
BALL

CUE
BALL

157.5°

© 1989
CHRIS
RAFTIS

57

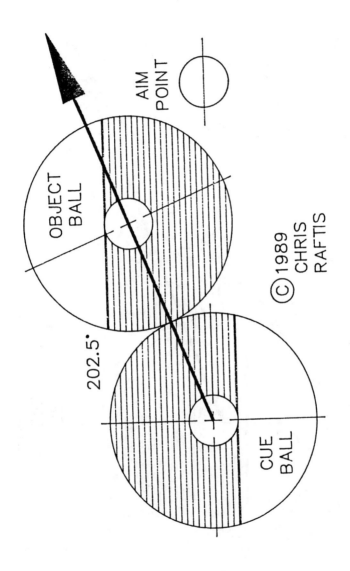

AIM
POINT

OBJECT
BALL

202.5°

© 1989
CHRIS
RAFTIS

CUE
BALL

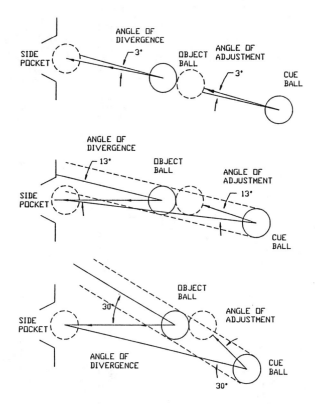

Examples of angle of deviation equals angle of adjustment

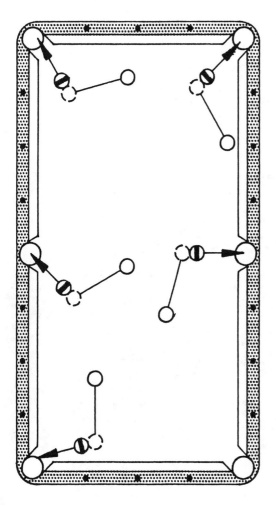

PRACTICE
SHOT SERIES

105° CUT
CUT SHOTS

FORCE
NO. 1 VERY SOFT

CUE BALL
HIT POINT

ANGLE OF CUE

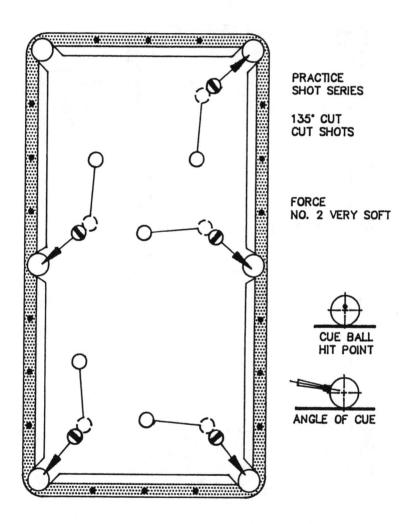

PRACTICE
SHOT SERIES

135° CUT
CUT SHOTS

FORCE
NO. 2 VERY SOFT

CUE BALL
HIT POINT

ANGLE OF CUE

61

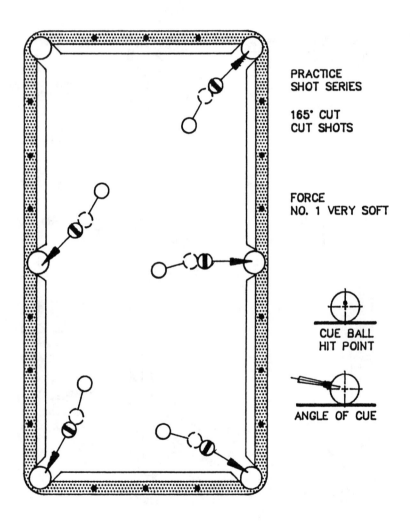

PRACTICE
SHOT SERIES

165° CUT
CUT SHOTS

FORCE
NO. 1 VERY SOFT

CUE BALL
HIT POINT

ANGLE OF CUE

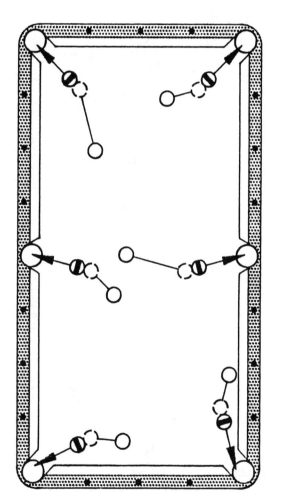

PRACTICE
SHOT SERIES

210° CUT
CUT SHOTS

FORCE
NO. 2 VERY SOFT

CUE BALL
HIT POINT

ANGLE OF CUE

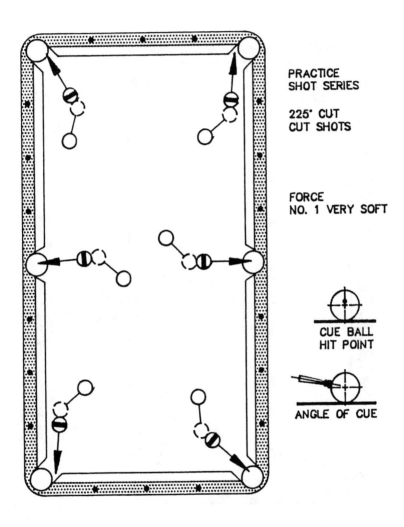

PRACTICE
SHOT SERIES

225° CUT
CUT SHOTS

FORCE
NO. 1 VERY SOFT

CUE BALL
HIT POINT

ANGLE OF CUE

64

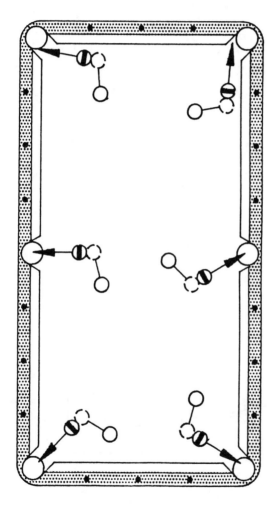

PRACTICE
SHOT SERIES

255° CUT
CUT SHOTS

FORCE
NO. 1 VERY SOFT

CUE BALL
HIT POINT

ANGLE OF CUE

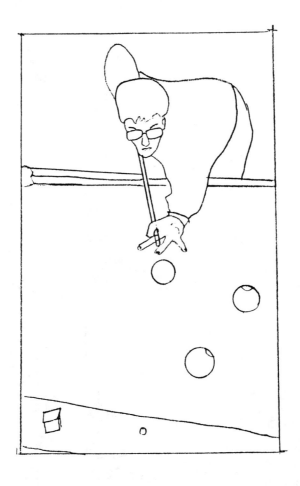

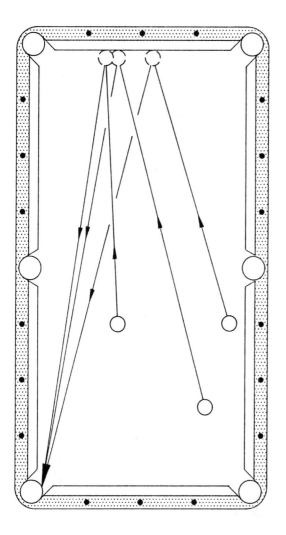

∠ Incidence =
∠ Reflection

ONE RAIL
into the
CORNER

FORCE:
NO. 5 MEDIUM

CUE BALL
HIT POINT

ANGLE OF CUE

67

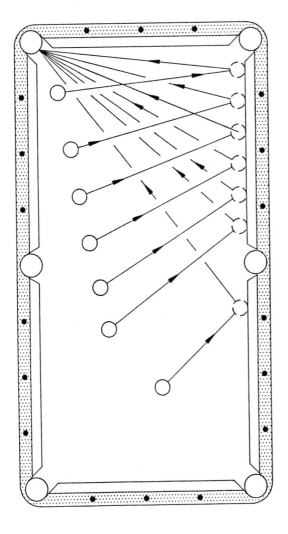

Practice
Shot Series

PLAYING
thru the
DIAMONDS

FORCE:
NO. 3 SOFT

CUE BALL
HIT POINT

ANGLE OF CUE

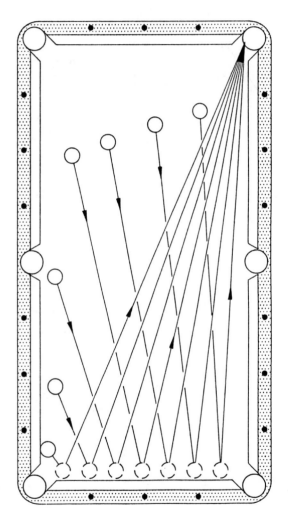

PRACTICE SHOT

PLAYING THROUGH
THE DIAMONDS

FORCE:
NO. 5 MEDIUM

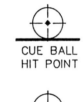

CUE BALL
HIT POINT

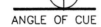

ANGLE OF CUE

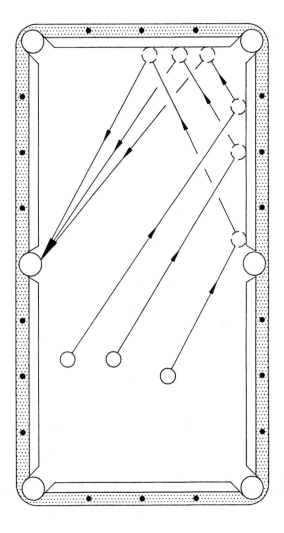

∠ Incidence =
  ∠ Reflection

TWO RAILS
into the
SIDE POCKET

FORCE:
NO. 4 SOFT

CUE BALL
HIT POINT

ANGLE OF CUE

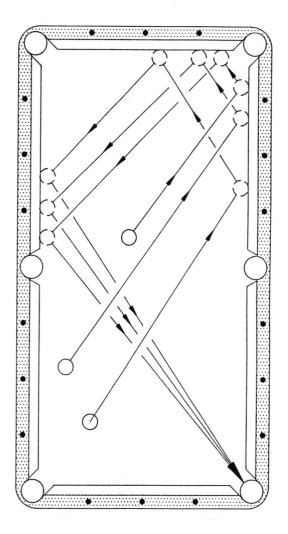

∠ Incidence =
∠ Reflection

THREE RAILS
into the
CORNER

FORCE:
NO. 5 MEDIUM

CUE BALL
HIT POINT

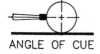

ANGLE OF CUE

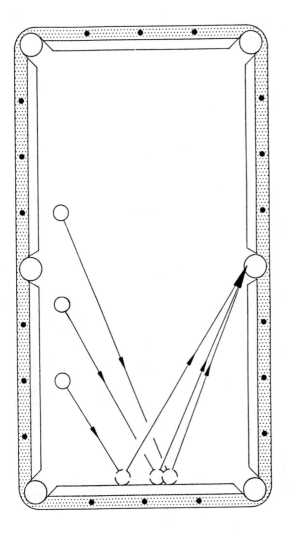

∠ Incidence =
∠ Reflection

ONE RAIL
into the
SIDE POCKET

FORCE:
NO. 3 SOFT

CUE BALL
HIT POINT

ANGLE OF CUE

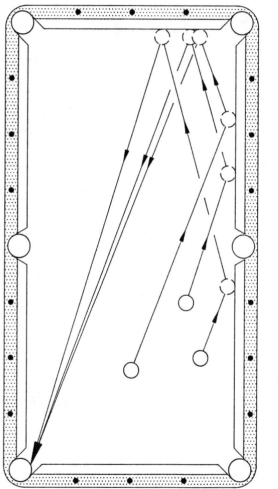

∠ Incidence =
∠ Reflection

TWO RAILS
into the
CORNER

FORCE:
NO. 4 SOFT

CUE BALL
HIT POINT

ANGLE OF CUE

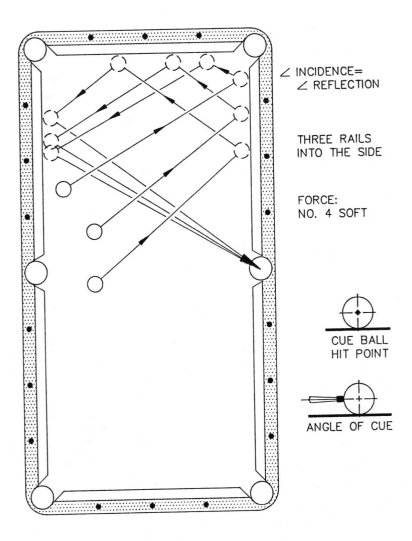

∠ INCIDENCE=
∠ REFLECTION

THREE RAILS
INTO THE SIDE

FORCE:
NO. 4 SOFT

CUE BALL
HIT POINT

ANGLE OF CUE

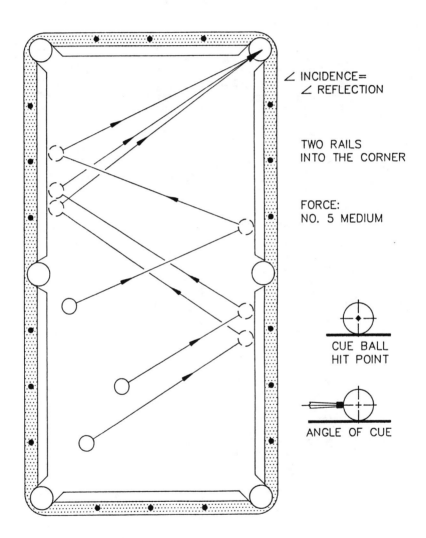

∠ INCIDENCE=
∠ REFLECTION

TWO RAILS
INTO THE CORNER

FORCE:
NO. 5 MEDIUM

CUE BALL
HIT POINT

ANGLE OF CUE

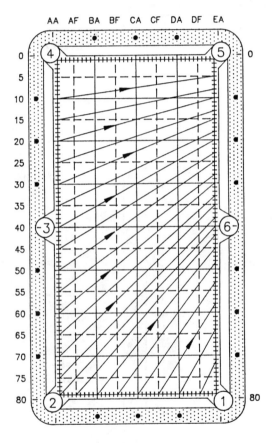

BANK SHOT

One rail
across corner

Force: 3–4

Cue ball hit
in center

Angle of cue
level

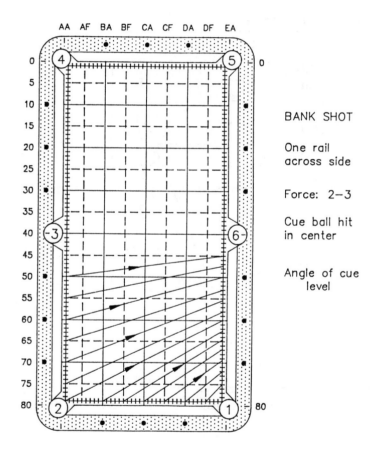

BANK SHOT

One rail
across side

Force: 2–3

Cue ball hit
in center

Angle of cue
level

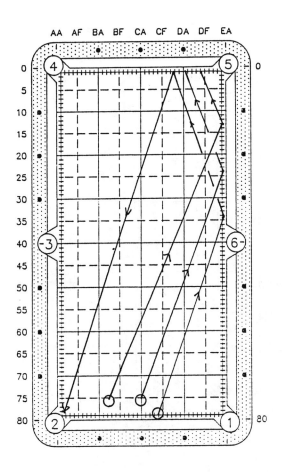

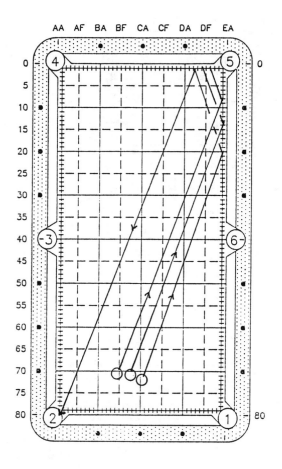

79

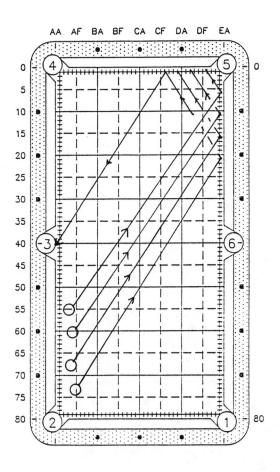

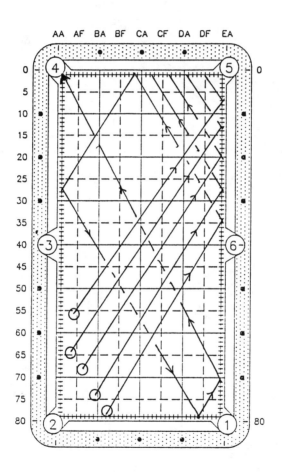

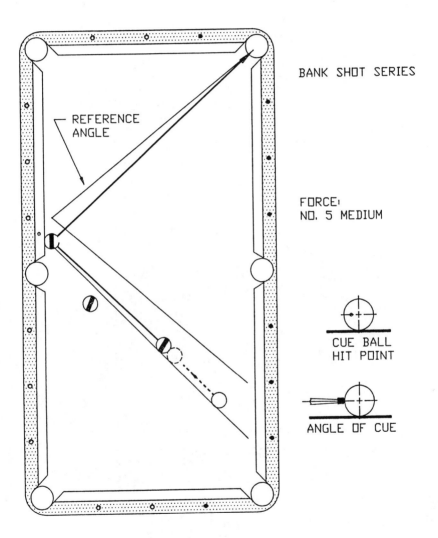

BANK SHOT SERIES

REFERENCE ANGLE

FORCE:
NO. 5 MEDIUM

CUE BALL
HIT POINT

ANGLE OF CUE

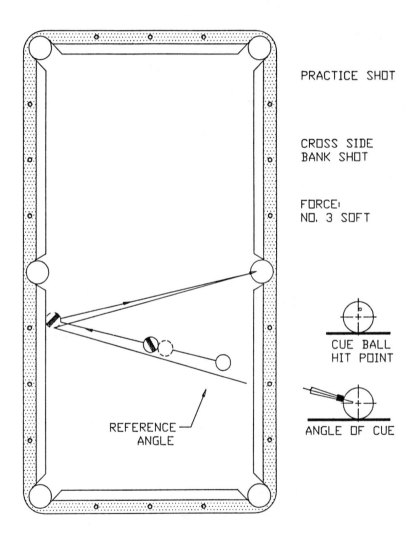

PRACTICE SHOT

CROSS SIDE
BANK SHOT

FORCE:
NO. 3 SOFT

CUE BALL
HIT POINT

ANGLE OF CUE

REFERENCE
ANGLE

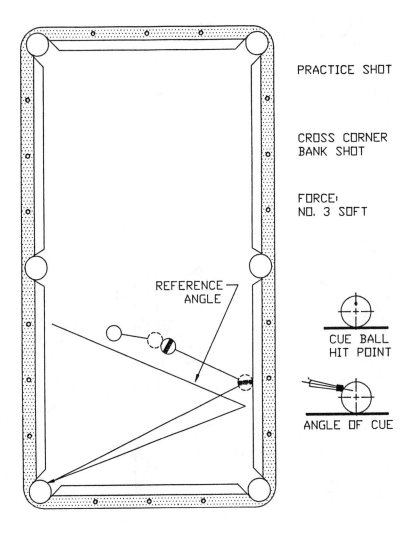

PRACTICE SHOT

CROSS CORNER
BANK SHOT

FORCE:
NO. 3 SOFT

REFERENCE
ANGLE

CUE BALL
HIT POINT

ANGLE OF CUE

84

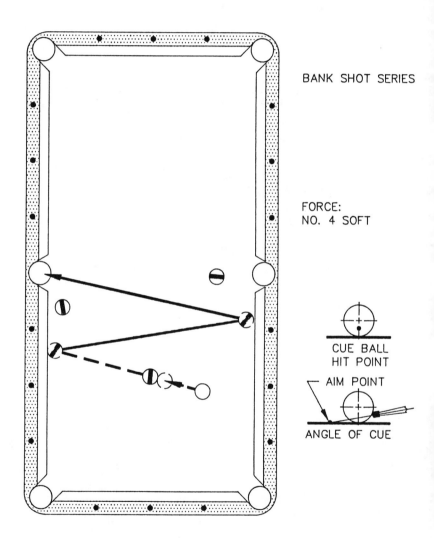

BANK SHOT SERIES

FORCE:
NO. 4 SOFT

CUE BALL
HIT POINT

AIM POINT

ANGLE OF CUE

85

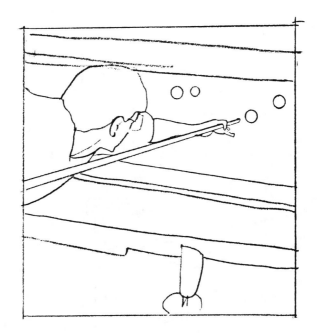

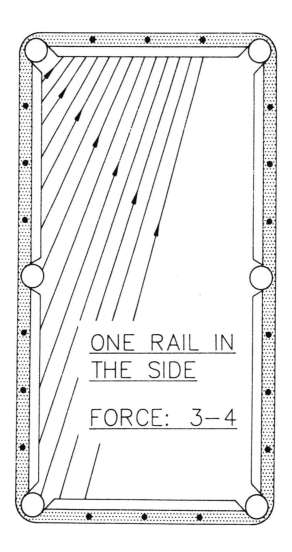

ONE RAIL IN
THE SIDE

FORCE: 3—4

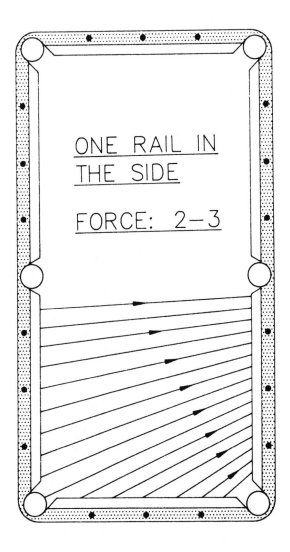

ONE RAIL IN
THE SIDE

FORCE: 2-3

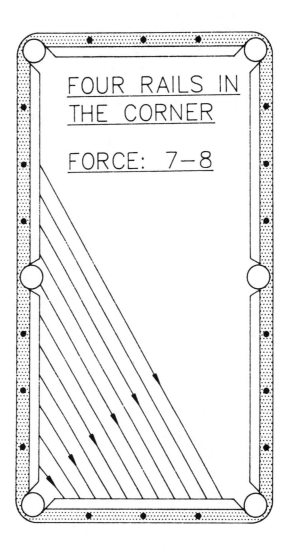

FOUR RAILS IN
THE CORNER

FORCE: 7–8

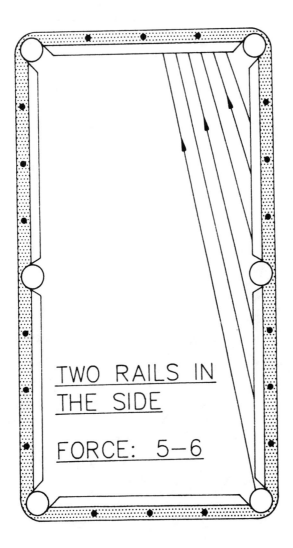

TWO RAILS IN
THE SIDE

FORCE: 5-6

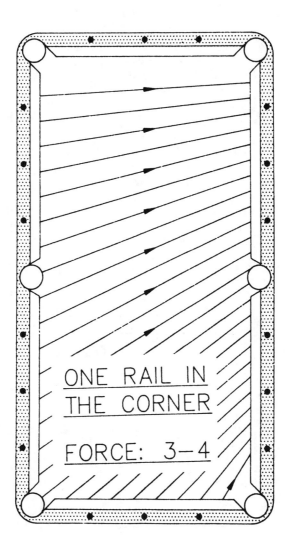

ONE RAIL IN
THE CORNER

FORCE: 3-4

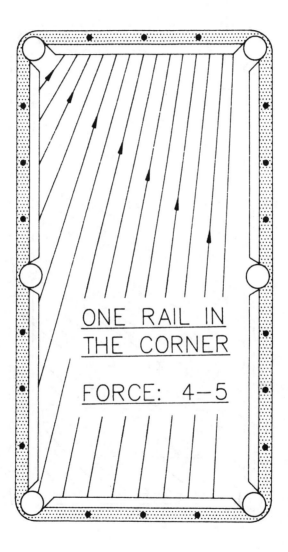

ONE RAIL IN
THE CORNER

FORCE: 4−5

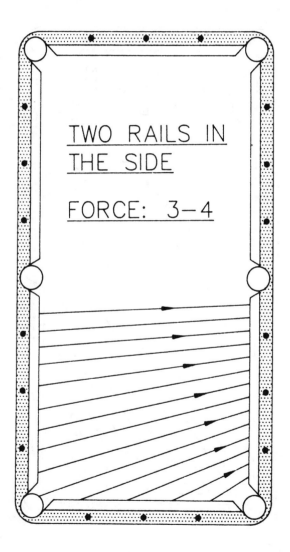

TWO RAILS IN
THE SIDE

FORCE: 3−4

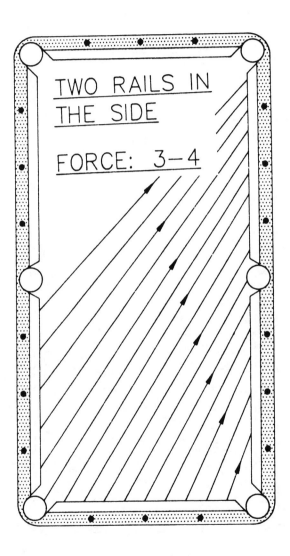

TWO RAILS IN
THE SIDE

FORCE: 3-4

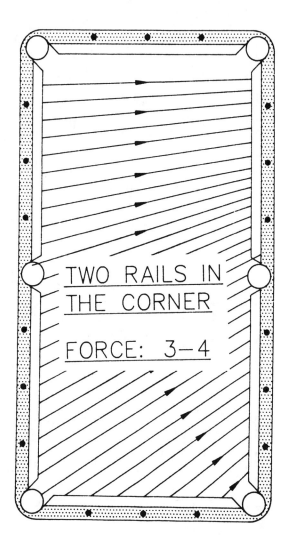

TWO RAILS IN THE CORNER

FORCE: 3—4

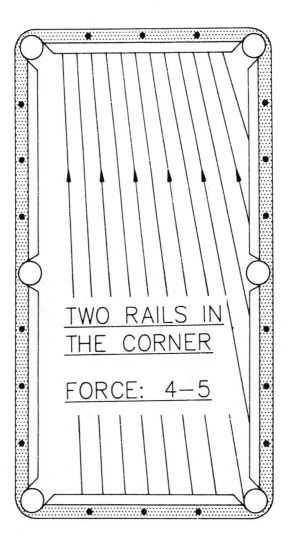

TWO RAILS IN
THE CORNER

FORCE: 4-5

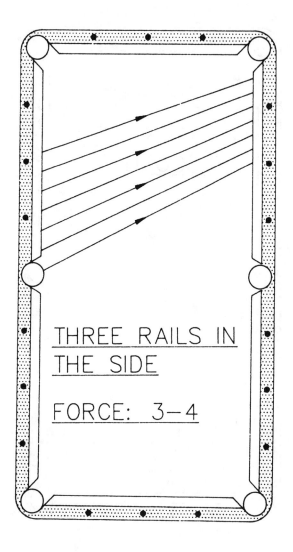

THREE RAILS IN
THE SIDE

FORCE: 3-4

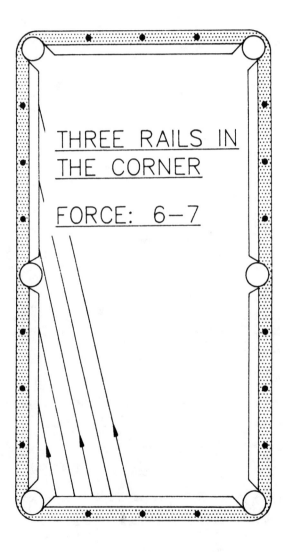

THREE RAILS IN
THE CORNER

FORCE: 6-7

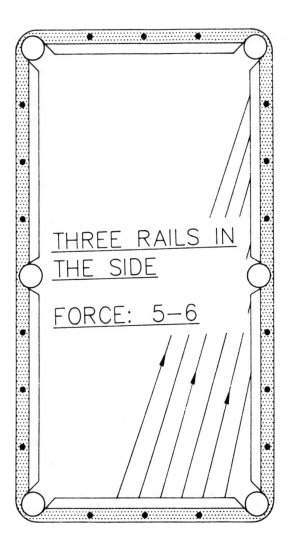

THREE RAILS IN
THE SIDE

FORCE: 5-6

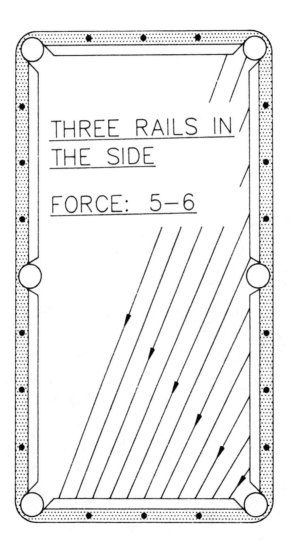

THREE RAILS IN
THE SIDE

FORCE: 5—6

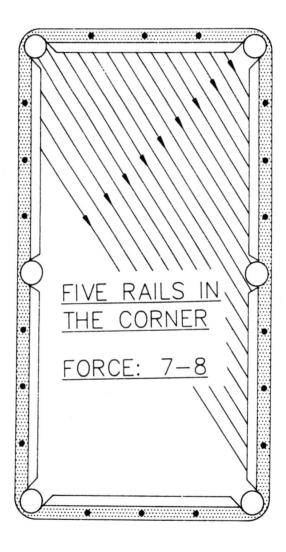

FIVE RAILS IN
THE CORNER

FORCE: 7—8

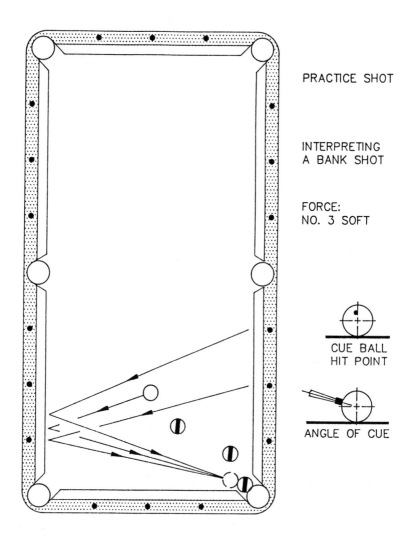

PRACTICE SHOT

INTERPRETING
A BANK SHOT

FORCE:
NO. 3 SOFT

CUE BALL
HIT POINT

ANGLE OF CUE

103

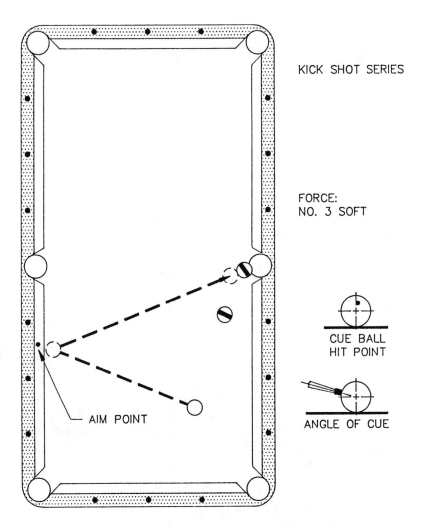

KICK SHOT SERIES

FORCE:
NO. 3 SOFT

CUE BALL
HIT POINT

ANGLE OF CUE

AIM POINT

104

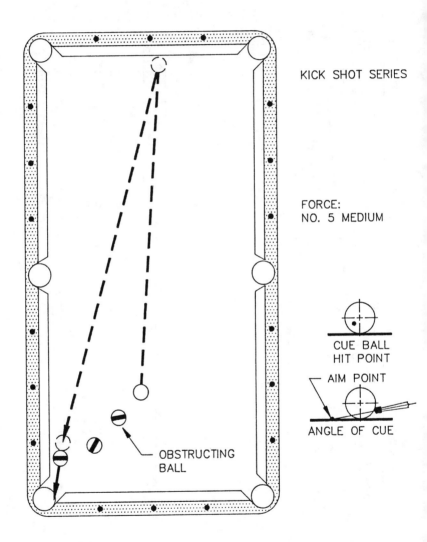

KICK SHOT SERIES

FORCE:
NO. 5 MEDIUM

CUE BALL
HIT POINT

AIM POINT

ANGLE OF CUE

OBSTRUCTING
BALL

105

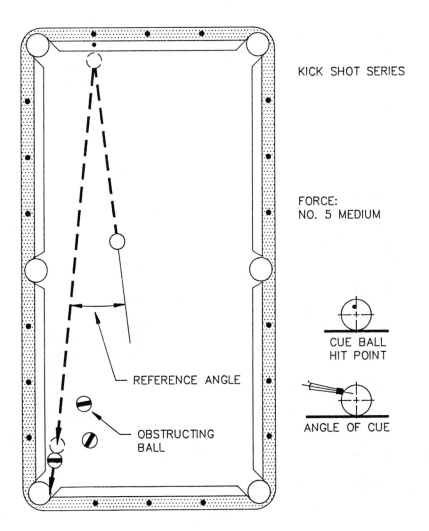

KICK SHOT SERIES

FORCE:
NO. 5 MEDIUM

CUE BALL
HIT POINT

ANGLE OF CUE

REFERENCE ANGLE

OBSTRUCTING
BALL

106

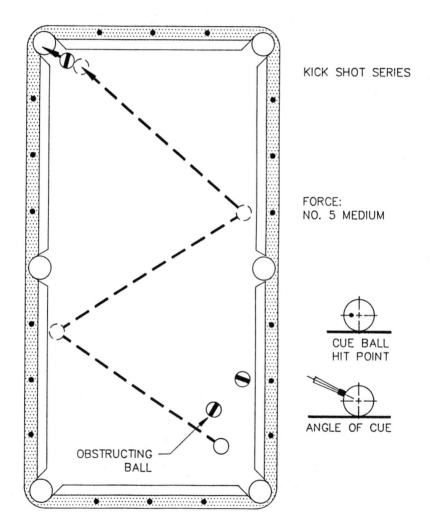

KICK SHOT SERIES

FORCE:
NO. 5 MEDIUM

CUE BALL
HIT POINT

ANGLE OF CUE

OBSTRUCTING
BALL

107

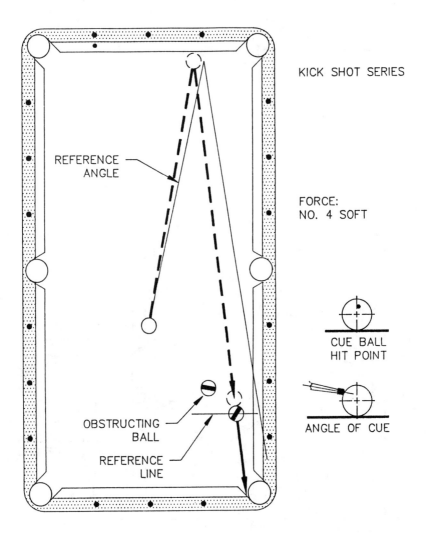

KICK SHOT SERIES

FORCE:
NO. 4 SOFT

CUE BALL
HIT POINT

ANGLE OF CUE

REFERENCE
ANGLE

OBSTRUCTING
BALL

REFERENCE
LINE

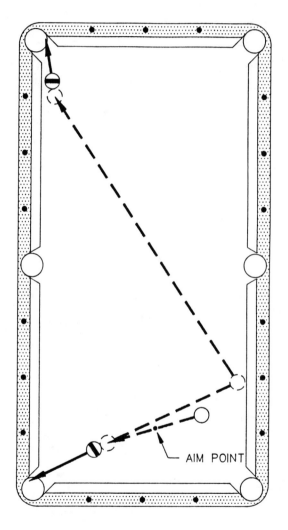

KICK SHOT SERIES

FORCE:
NO. 5 MEDIUM

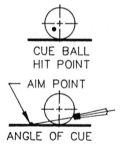

CUE BALL
HIT POINT

AIM POINT

ANGLE OF CUE

AIM POINT

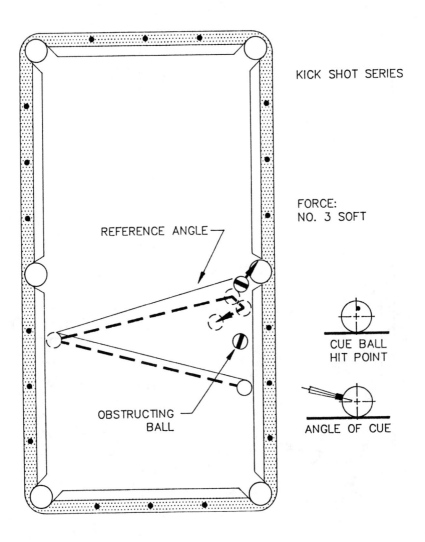

KICK SHOT SERIES

FORCE:
NO. 3 SOFT

REFERENCE ANGLE

OBSTRUCTING
BALL

CUE BALL
HIT POINT

ANGLE OF CUE

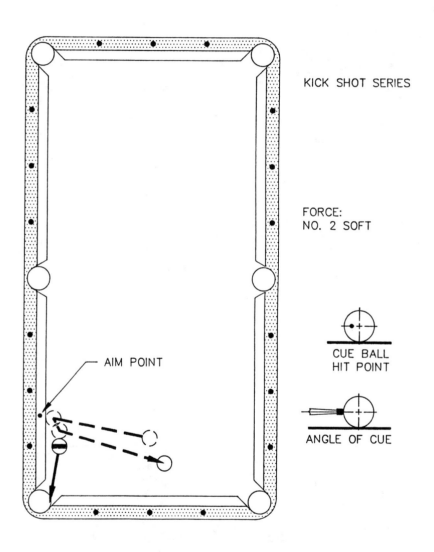

KICK SHOT SERIES

FORCE:
NO. 2 SOFT

CUE BALL
HIT POINT

ANGLE OF CUE

AIM POINT

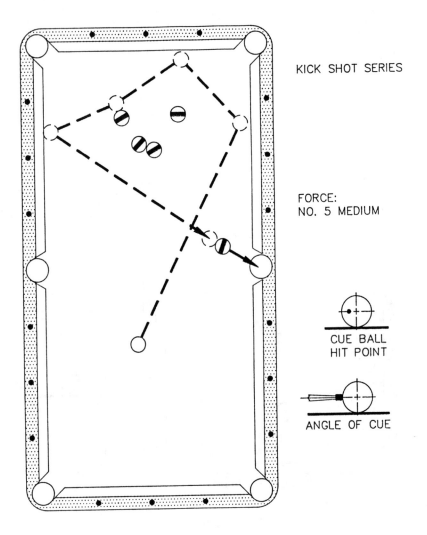

KICK SHOT SERIES

FORCE:
NO. 5 MEDIUM

CUE BALL
HIT POINT

ANGLE OF CUE

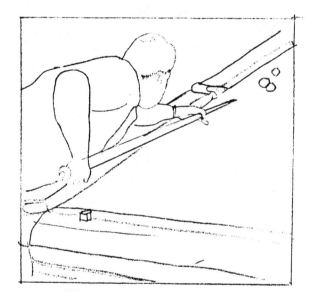

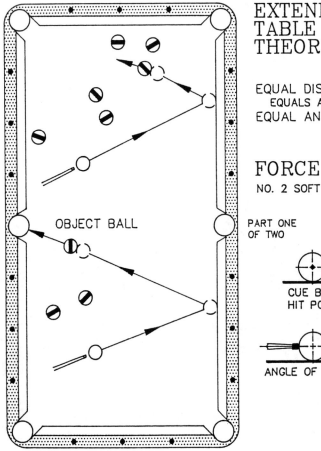

EXTENDED TABLE THEORY

EQUAL DISTANCE
EQUALS AN
EQUAL ANGLE

FORCE
NO. 2 SOFT

PART ONE
OF TWO

OBJECT BALL

CUE BALL
HIT POINT

ANGLE OF CUE

114

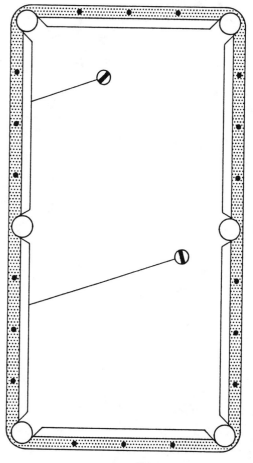

EXTENDED TABLE THEORY

BALLS
PROJECTED
ON AN
IMAGINARY
TABLE

PART TWO

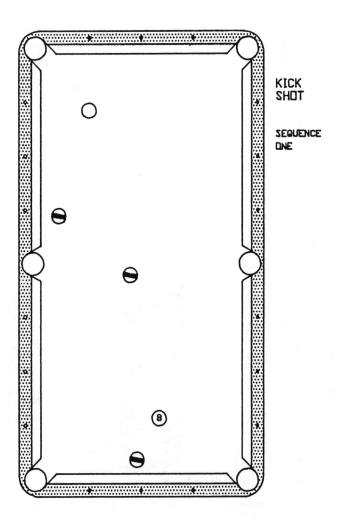

KICK
SHOT

SEQUENCE
ONE

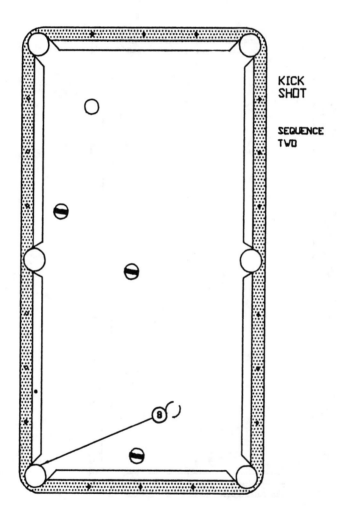

KICK
SHOT

SEQUENCE
TWO

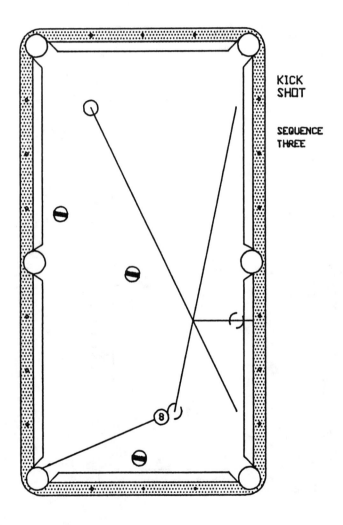

KICK
SHOT

SEQUENCE
THREE

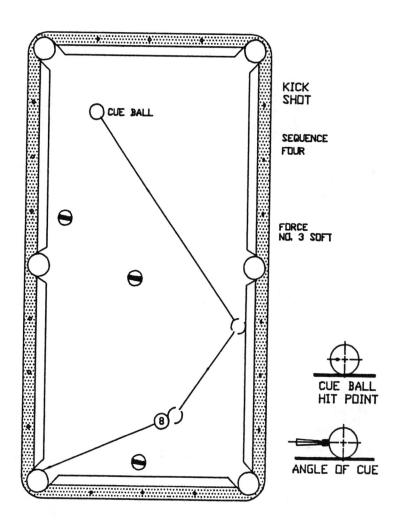

KICK
SHOT

SEQUENCE
FOUR

FORCE
NO. 3 SOFT

CUE BALL

CUE BALL
HIT POINT

ANGLE OF CUE

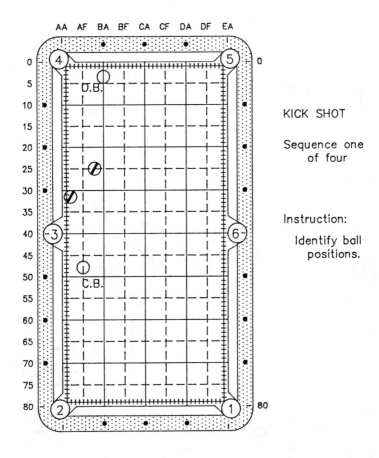

KICK SHOT

Sequence one
of four

Instruction:

Identify ball
positions.

120

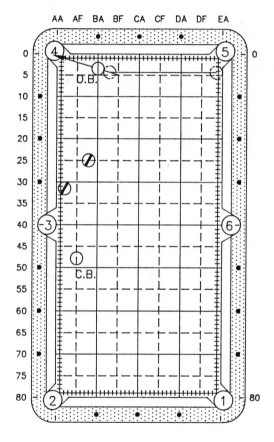

KICK SHOT

Sequence two
    of four

Instruction:

Measure distance
between centers
of phantom cue
ball and imaginary
ball touching rail.

121

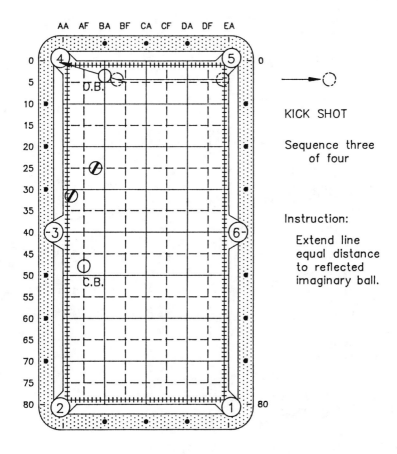

KICK SHOT

Sequence three
of four

Instruction:

Extend line
equal distance
to reflected
imaginary ball.

122

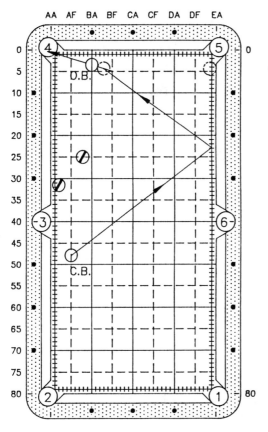

KICK SHOT

Sequence four
of four

Instruction:

Aim cue ball
for reflected
phantom cue
ball. Strike
cue ball in
center and use
force number
three.

123

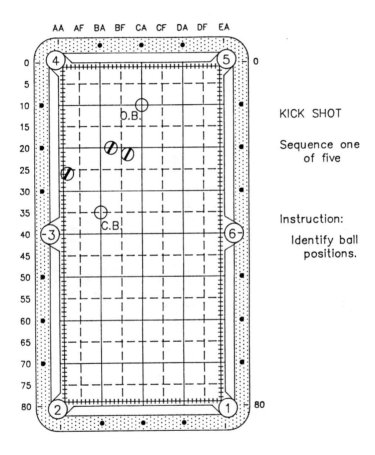

KICK SHOT

Sequence one
of five

Instruction:

Identify ball
positions.

124

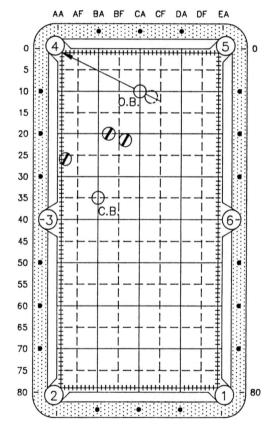

KICK SHOT

Sequence two
of five

Instruction:

Locate the
position of the
phantom cue ball.

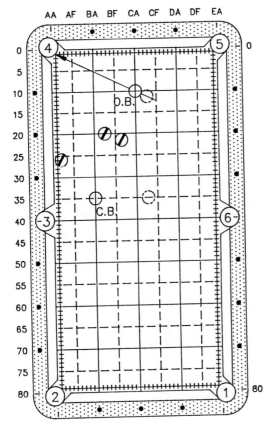

KICK SHOT

Sequence three
of five

Instruction:

Align imaginary
cue ball with
phantom cue
ball in a line
with actual
cue ball.

126

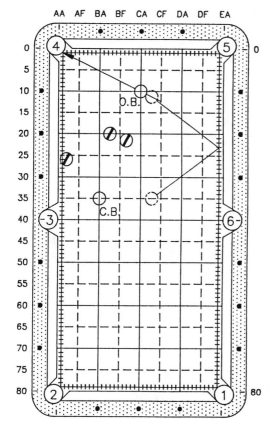

KICK SHOT

Sequence four
   of five

Instruction:

   Produce equal
   angle by dividing
   distance along
   rail as shown.

127

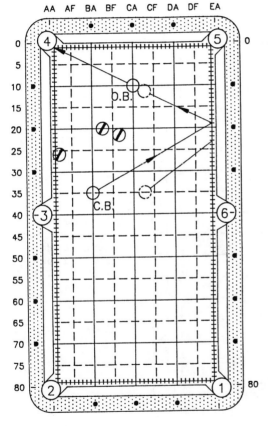

KICK SHOT

Sequence five
of five

Instruction:

Straight line
from imaginary
cue ball to
rail and strike
cue ball in
center and use
force number
three.

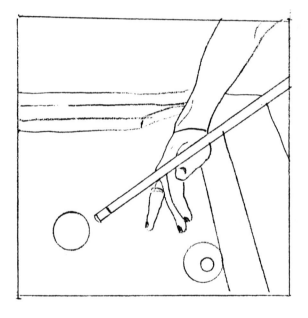

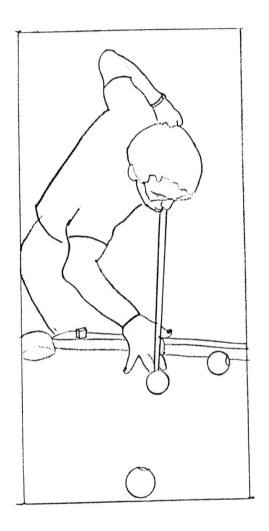

130

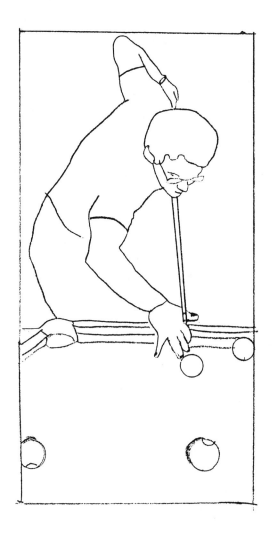

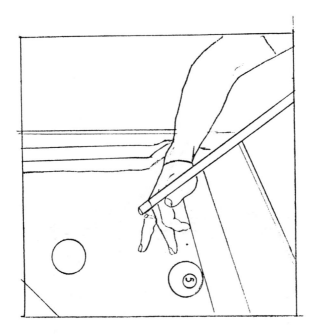

The games

A. NINE BALL.

In the game of nine ball it is very important to develop a good break shot. In order to execute a good break shot, the cue stick should accelerate rapidly with some forward body movement. In order to have a good impact and large ball movement it is necessary that the apex ball be struck full face. A well hit cue ball should travel at approximately twenty five miles per hour for a male player and twenty miles an hour for a female player.

One object on the break shot could be to pocket the apex ball in the side pocket. This is done by striking the cue ball below center and striking the object ball off center to the outside. It would help to strike the cue ball slightly off center to the inside of the hit. If executed successfully the apex ball will rebound from the rack into the side pocket. This is not a sure thing but with practice you may get a good percentage and if not the seldom ball will help to win a game.

Another method of striking the rack is to strike the apex ball across the face with a cue ball struck above center. The result is that on a few occasions the cue ball will rebound from the rail and kick in the nine ball into the corner pocket. Kicking another ball in is also a possibility.

The game of nine ball is played by racking nine balls numbered consecutively from one through nine into a diamond shape with the one ball as the apex ball and the nine ball or striped ball in the center of the racked balls. The tighter the rack the better the distribution of balls on the break. After the break shot the object balls are struck in consecutive order until the nine ball is pocketed, which ends the game.

One variation of play is that the five ball becomes a second principal object ball and is placed at the end of the rack.

Another variation of play is that
the nine ball must be pocketed as
the last ball to complete the game;
therefore, each time the nine ball
is pocketed previous to the last
ball is a win.

One condition of play in nine ball
is that when a foul is committed
the cue ball is in hand, meaning
that you are allowed to pick up the
cue ball and place it wherever it
suits your best interests. A foul
means to pocket the cue ball; move
a ball accidentally; to not strike
a rail after contacting an object
ball; or to jump the cue ball off
the table.

The one exception to this rule is
on the break shot. If a foul is
committed on the break shot then
the cue ball is placed behind the
head string or a line drawn across
the table from the second diamond
position.

Many players like to play "all
balls down stay down", which means
that if you have the cue ball in
hand after the break shot and your
desired object ball is behind the

head string then that ball is
pocketed by hand and you strike on
the next ball. Also if the cue
ball enters a pocket after an
object ball is pocketed, the object
ball remains pocketed unless it is
the nine ball. The same rule is
true if the cue ball jumps the
table after pocketing an object
ball. If an object ball is pocketed
accidentally by hand then that ball
also would remain pocketed unless
it was the nine ball. If the nine
ball has to be placed on the table
after illegal pocketing then it
should be replaced at the
approximate position it occupied
previous or be placed on the foot
spot.

Sometimes "pushes" are allowed. An
example of a "push" is as follows:
when there are obstructing balls
between the cue ball and the
desired object ball then you may
take the side of the cue near the
tip and strike the cue ball so that
the cue ball is in the "open" or so
that the path between the cue ball
and the desired object ball is
clear. The incoming player then has
a choice; either to shoot or allow

you to shoot.   A push is   normally
allowed on the   shot following   the
break shot.

If you cannot make all the balls in
consecutive order, then it   becomes
necessary to play a safety.   There
are several ways to play a   safety.
First   there   is   a   "snooker".   A
"snooker" means that   the cue   ball
or desired object ball   is   behind
another ball or group of balls.   In
other words   one   of the   balls   is
hidden so   that direct   contact   is
not possible.   To   get   out   of   a
snooker it is necessary to play one
of the following shots: a curve;   a
bank; or a jump.

Second   there   is   the   "lag".   By
striking the object   ball thin   and
with a   soft force,   you can   "lag"
the cue ball   to the farthest   rail
or a   nearby   rail,   hoping for   a
freeze on the rail.   The shot   then
becomes more difficult because   you
can only strike the cue ball   above
center with   an   elevated   cue   and
distance between the   cue ball   and
the desired object ball helps   make
the shot more difficult.

Third is to strike the object ball so that it travels to a rail hoping for a freeze.

Fourth is to strike the object ball so that when it stops your opponent will be left with a difficult shot.

When playing at nine ball it is always necessary to read the table, which means to plan ahead as many shots as is practical. Every player does not read the table the same; therefore what is correct for one player may not be correct for another player. Although in many situations the same or a similar pattern will develop.

One method of playing position is to leave the cue ball near the object ball and the shortest distance from the previous object ball.

Another style of play is to play the speed of the cue ball for position on the second object ball. In other words you make a normal cut shot but by utilizing more or less speed on the cue ball you

arrive at a favored position for
the next shot.

One strategy is to always play to
score the sure shots and play safe
on a difficult shot.

The idea of strategy is to
visualize how you can score your
shots and at the same time make it
difficult for your opponent to
score his shots.

A definition of a legal shot is
that you struck a desired object
ball after which the desired object
ball or the cue ball contacted a
rail or you pocketed an object
ball.

The exception to this rule is when
the object ball is frozen or
touching the cushion, then it
becomes necessary to contact
another cushion with the cue ball
or object ball.

Many nine ball matches are played
as a run to seven. instead of seven
it could be a run to nine, eleven
or any other number. A run to a
number means that when a player

wins the specified number of games then he wins the match. Sometimes this activity is known as a "freeze out".

When playing a "freeze out" the player who is able to gain the lead could be called a "front runner". A "front runner" may be able to take more risks than the player who is behind. An example would be that a "front runner" when faced with a difficult shot pattern that would normally require playing a safety would "shoot out" for a score instead, hoping to increase the win total and the match.

Many players will tell you that your best defense is a good offense.

Along these same lines some tournament conductors and players like to use the rule that three fouls during a game becomes a loss of the game. A variation of this rule is that the three fouls need to be successive shots. After the offending player has committed two fouls, his opponent must warn him of the foul trouble before the opportunity to commit the third foul.

One strategy when playing against a "front runner" is to try to increase the amount of safeties that you play so as to wear him down and not give him an opportunity for "striking out" or "running out".

The same strategy can be applied towards a player who enjoys "shooting out". "Shooting out" and "running out" are similar terminology. A "shoot out" player tries to score all the shots in succession and doesn't attempt safety play. This style of player is most difficult to defeat. When he is "on his game" you might say that he is impossible to defeat.

When "reading the table" it is good to know what your shot percentages are in order to determine if you will go all out for the shot; play easy position; hard position; a half safety; or a full safety. Your judgement should be based on how well you are able to score the shot in front of you.

One consideration when "reading the table" is at what point does the percentage shot appear· in the game. If a low percentage shot appears as the final shot in the game you may want to go for it. If the same shot appears early in the game you would probably play a safety.

Another example would be that if you have been practicing difficult cut shots into the corner pocket using a mechanical bridge and you have scored six out of nine shots then your chances of scoring would be two to one in your favor. So if the game is a close match you might not want to take the chance of the miss. Of course if you are in front in the match the risk might not be as great; also if your opponent is a much weaker player then the risk also would not be as great.

Many times you will need to plan several shots ahead. In this way you will be able to plan how to break out clusters from the rail to improve the shot making opportunities.

The more knowledge you have about bank angles and cut shots the easier it is to play out of trouble; such as making a kick shot when you are snookered.

On occasion it may be advisable to pocket a ball out of sequence; such as, when the nine ball is in or near a pocket and you don't have a good scoring opportunity.

The game is started by each player lagging a ball to the starting rail and the ball closest to the rail wins the lag.

Another method of starting is to call on the flip of a coin. The last method is to concede the start to the weaker player.

When you become a strong nine ball player you may have to spot a ball or balls to make a game. First you would spot the eight ball, which means that any time during the game that your opponent pockets the eight ball he wins the game. If you have difficulty making a game spotting the eight ball then you can add a seven ball spot. If there

is still difficulty then you have
to give the break shot in addition.
This is the limit that you can give
in a nine ball match. If you still
cannot make a match then you have
to give a game concession; such as
you play to seven games for the
match while your opponent plays to
five games.

B. EIGHT BALL

Actually the statistics are not
available but as more home tables
are sold eight ball will be the
most popular game. I am hoping that
you are already familiar with the
general play of eight ball so I
will go over the highlights.

Seven of the object balls have a
colored band and these are called
the "stripes". Seven of the other
balls are a solid color and these
are called the "solids". One ball
is black and is called the eight
ball. The game can also be played
with seven balls of one color;
seven balls of another color; and a
black ball.

144

The break shot is determined by lagging two object balls; tossing a coin; ;or by the stronger player relinquishing the shot to the weaker player. After the first break shot, the succeeding break shots are determined by who wins the game.

If a ball is not pocketed on the break shot, the incoming player may elect to shoot at the stripes or solids, whichever will give the best advantage. The choice is always with the incoming player until a ball is pocketed, then that player must continue pocketing all the balls of that set and his opponent then must pocket the other balls. If you pocket your opponents' ball by mistake or intentionally then that ball remains pocketed to your opponents' advantage.

If the cue ball scratches while pocketing one or more balls in your set, then those balls are spotted on the foot spot where the apex ball was placed when the balls were racked.

The fifteen balls are racked with the apex ball on the foot spot and the eight ball in the center of the rack. The other balls are mixed in the rack.

A good percentage can be had by playing the apex ball into the side pocket. Place the cue ball about a diamond up from the short rail and about a half diamond in from the long rail on either side of the table. Strike the apex ball just off center to the outside with the cue ball. Strike the cue ball just off center to the inside and low using a hard force to break the rack. Another method of breaking the rack is to strike the apex ball straight on with the strongest force possible.

If the eight ball is pocketed previous to the pocketing of the set of seven balls then the player pocketing the eight ball loses the game. If you pocket the eight ball and then scratch the cue ball then you lose the game. Another rule that some players use is when you are striking on the eight ball and you fail to hit the eight ball you lose the game.

When playing at eight ball there is no fixed consecutive order of shots; therefore the opportunity for scoring is greater than in nine ball.

The object of the game of eight ball is to pocket the required eight balls before your opponent pockets his balls. If you are faced with a difficult shot in the sequence then you would want to play a safety. If your opponent has a ball in the pocket opening from which he can get easy position for the next shot and may run out, then you may want to forfeit your turn at the table by pocketing the ball and leaving your opponent with a difficult shot.

If you are faced with a difficult shot then you will want to play safe or defensive. One method is to hide the cue ball behind an object ball. Another is to leave the cue ball as close to a rail as possible. Last is to knock your opponents'object ball away from the pocket opening.

When you read the table for a run out, you must select the principal ball or the seventh object ball so that you are able to secure good position on the eight ball. So the way you do this is to see where the position of the eight ball is and then try to find the seventh object ball. If when reading the table you are unable to locate the seventh object ball then you might want to consider playing a safety instead of going for a score.

In order to make a game with a weaker player, you might want to spot two object balls after the break shot. You need to always have the break shot when making this offer. When you select the two balls for your opponent, you will want to consider if the selected balls are to be used offensively or defensively. In other words you take two balls that will clear your seven balls or you take two balls that your opponent would have scored anyway. One other alternative is to leave your

opponent safe by removing two balls
that are in easy striking distance
or by not removing balls that are
near your opponents' cue ball, so
as to leave him a difficult scoring
position. Sometimes it is easier to
win by giving your opponent a spot
of two balls because automatically
the nature of the game is changed
and you exercise more control over
the results.

Some variations of rules when
playing eight ball are:

To pocket the eight ball in the
same pocket as the seventh ball.

To pocket the one ball in the side
pocket if you have the solids or
to pocket the fifteen ball in the
other side pocket if you have the
stripes.

To bank the eight ball on a called
shot.

Different players and lounges have
their own rules. Check first before
playing.

C. EIGHT BALL PLAYED WITH NINE BALLS.

The balls are racked in a diamond shape with four striped balls; four solid color balls; and the eight ball in the center. The balls are mixed in the rack. The game is played as outlined previously. Three advantages can be noted. One is the ease of the break shot. Another is there are less clusters. The last consideration is the time element. Eight ball with nine balls takes about half the time and therefore allows more games to be played in the same amount of time.

D. SIX BALL PLAYED WITH A SPECIAL FIVE BALL.

The balls are racked in a pyramid shape with the five ball in the middle of the back row. The five other balls can be of any denomination as they only count for one point each when pocketed. The five ball is special and counts for five points.

Three shots are allowed each player to pocket the six balls. The number of players does not have to be limited. The break shot is a free shot. If all the balls are scored from the break shot then there is a bonus of ten points plus the score of the next three shots. If all the balls are scored by the completion of the second shot then there is a bonus of ten points plus the score of the next two shots in the next rack. If all the balls are scored by the completion of the third shot then there is a bonus of ten points plus the score of the next shot in the next rack. If all the balls are not pocketed by the completion of the third shot then the total amount of points is recorded as a score for that turn at the table. Ten turns at the table are recommended. Different tables may be used by the players or more than one table may be used to facilitate the playing of the game. An early objective would be to pocket the five ball for the five points.

This game easily allows handicapping and ranking of players on a local, regional and national level.

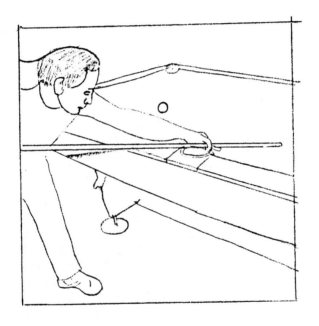

Position play

One method of playing position is to position the cue ball for a series of draw shots. You draw the cue ball by striking the cue ball below center and through the ball to a point on the cloth beyond the cue ball. Use a quick wrist motion for the best results.

Another method of playing position is to strike the cue ball near the center and move the cue ball the shortest distance towards the desired object ball and in a direction where the object ball would be the shortest distance to the pocket.

A more difficult way of playing position is to try to play the cue ball to come to rest as close to the object ball as practical. This would require the use of various spins on the cue ball and may result in a greater percentage of missed shots.

Another method of position play is to play only the speed of the cue ball for position.

Last is to use all the above
techniques according to which give
you the best advantage.

One bit of advice is to not
sacrifice pocketing the ball in
order to get good position, but
always try a little harder to get
position when pocketing a ball. Do
not neglect the need for good
position just to score a ball. See
diagrams.

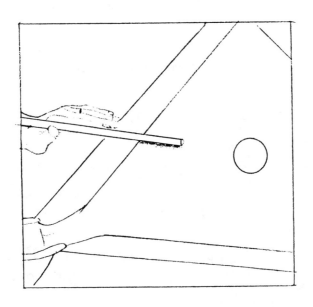

Competition

A. In order to compete you must be mentally and physically prepared. To be mentally prepared you need to be able to concentrate, which means to place only one thought or object in the minds' eye at one time. Mental discipline is required. This can be obtained by mental exercises such as adding numbers mentally instead of physically. There are other mental exercises such as remembering or memorizing shot patterns. Mental stability is necessary, which means that you should be peaceful and your home situation should be stable. The ability to make good judgements is necessary. These judgements are based on experiences. You must be mentally alert and attentive. Physically you should have stamina and good eyesight. You should be comfortable and not tense. You must be determined to win or play your best. Patience is a virtue worth cultivating. When your opponent is shooting the only thing that you can do is to be patient and wait your turn. You must stay composed and not become disturbed while

awaiting your turn at the table.
And even while playing you do not
want to become disturbed by missed
shots or scratches. In other words
you should be at your best
performance while competing, both
mentally and physically.

B. Strategy: Before you can plan
your strategy you need to know your
opponents' weak and strong points.
I will list the different players'
styles that you have to consider:

1. An aggressive player who shoots
at all shots. This player is very
difficult to defeat when he is on
his game. Seeing how he will shoot
at anything you may be able to turn
the game around by playing
deliberate safeties. These safeties
will tend to slow him down plus
give you some excellent scoring
opportunities. Leave this player
many long thin shots, snookers, or
balls frozen against the rail. This
then is your best strategy.

2. Next is the safety player. If he
doesn't like the percentage shot,
he will play a deliberate safety.
In order to defeat such a player

you will also have to play safeties. You cannot shoot out at his safeties, because this would tire you out and give your opponent better scoring opportunities. So you must play safe. That means to leave your opponent snookered, or a ball against a rail, or a long thin cut shot.

3. Then there is the determined player. He will score a few balls then play safe. Again he will score a few balls and play safe. He is very difficult to defeat. Your only strategy is to run out the rack or play him at his own game. In other words you make a few balls and play safe. Again make some more balls and play safe. This may unnerve your opponent. If the opportunity arises, go for the run out. Sometimes your best defense is a strong offense.

4. Another type of player is the "front runner". He tries to get in front quickly and then increase his lead by taking risks at scoring. The "front runner" is almost impossible to defeat. He is a shoot out player and if you want to

compete it is best to compete on
his level. It is possible to slow
him down or put him off his game by
playing deliberate safeties. This
is time consuming and if you are
not an excellent safety player then
it may be to no avail.

5. Next is the hustler. He never
shows his true strength. He tries
to "milk" the game. In other words
he will try to take an advantage by
winning two out of three or three
out of five games. He tries to gain
an advantage over a period of time.
If you know that you are being
hustled, it is best to minimize
your losses by quitting or increase
your opportunities to win by
increasing the spot. One way to
identify a "hustler" is that he may
consistently come from behind by
running out the last balls on the
table. Another way is that most of
his shots are "lucky" shots. In
other words the object ball may be
almost straight in the corner but
he will play it three rails into a
different corner and if it goes in
he will exclaim "what good luck".
Also he may miss some easy shots

and leave you safe so that you will again leave him an easy shot.

C. PRACTICAL ADVICES

1. You have to be peaceful. You cannot be easily disturbed. You need to have patience. You need to persevere. In other words the game is not over until the last shot is completed. Or the match is not over until the last game is won. You need to concentrate on the immediate shot. Picture the completed shot in your mind. Predetermine the speed of the stroke and where the cue ball will be left. Play the object ball for the correct entry into the pocket. Try to have only one thought in your mind at one time. You have to believe in your own success.

2. You must practice bank and cut shots on a regular basis. Try to always increase your percentages of completion. Sometimes you are left with an unusual shot. Unusual shots also need to be practiced. Practice to control the speed of the cue ball. There is a diagram of the different ball speeds. Remember

when cutting an object ball that
the less the object ball is
contacted, the more the speed of
the cue ball. Begin by practicing
one half hour a day and try to
increase to two hours a day. One
eye will coordinate the body
functions with the shot at hand.
Use the right eye if you are left
handed and use the left eye if you
are right handed.

D. PLAN AHEAD

Try to make a plan when reading the
table. In other words try to
determine the sequence of shots
that you plan to make mentally.
After making a determination then
try to execute your plan. Remember
in executing your plan to
concentrate on making only one shot
at a time. If you always make the
next shot then you will
successfully make all the shots.
Try to visualize your plan. Look
for the pictures in the mind. Of
course the mind needs to be trained
to see the right pictures. It is
necessary when executing a shot
pattern to put a little more energy
into a proper execution to ensure

proper position. Don't just pocket the object ball without considering the position of the cue ball for the next shot.

E. FOOD INTAKE

Don't eat a heavy meal prior to the start of a match. A heavy meal can cause sluggish reactions. Try to consume a light meal or take several small intakes of food instead. This will keep the body light and the mind alert. For some players light refreshments could be only liquids or hard candies. Fasting from foods may increase mental awareness. Try to refrain from smoking and ask your opponent to not smoke at the table. This will reduce irritations to the eyes and throat. Also smoking by yourself or others can help to break your concentration on the immediate shot pattern.

F. PERSONAL ATTITUDE

1. The attitude that you should have towards your opponent is that you are engaged in a test or a battle and your opponent is your

enemy. That doesn't mean that your opponent is always your enemy. He is only your enemy during the contest. You don't want to think harshly about him. You want to realize that here is a battle and this is my opponent. He is my enemy and I want to do whatever is in my power to defeat him.

Always be a gentleman and be serious about playing the game of pocket billiards. Pocket billiards can be a lot of fun but it also can be a lot of hard work. Use your turn at the table for your best advantage. Try to minimize your mistakes. Usually the player who makes the most mistakes loses the game or the match. You should always endeavor to win every game and every match.

Your opponent may be your teacher or a friend but when the match starts you must take an impersonal attitude toward your opponent and try to win the match. You have to think that you have to win every game and make every shot. Always try to defeat your opponent by not letting him have a good shot or win one game.

2. What should be your attitude towards a crowd? If the crowd is friendly then that is to your advantage and you should enjoy a pleasing attitude. If there is a heckler in the crowd then you should develop an impersonal attitude. Remember that every turn at the table is an opportunity to win and if you concentrate on your winning strategy you will not notice the heckler.

An unfriendly crowd is one that is favorable towards your opponent. Here again the impersonal attitude has to come into play. Try to concentrate on the shot at hand and play one shot at a time. Try to show confidence in your game. Don't become upset or irrational towards an unfriendly crowd. Remember that these times will pass and if you perform well the crowd may turn in your favor.

MECHANICAL AIDS

A. You will find several pages of cut shot patterns. Every seven and one half degrees of the circumference of the ball will be one cut shot pattern. The direction and degrees can be reversed if necessary. Photocopy the page and cut out the individual templates. Make an indentation in the center of the object ball circle or place a half inch ring binder retainer inside the seventeen thirty seconds circle of the object ball drawing. This is necessary to spot the object ball accurately when the template is placed on the table. Place the template on the table and align the arrow head for the desired objective, either a hit point on the rail or a portion of a pocket opening. Place the cue ball on the table in a favorable position for making the shot pattern. Place a piece of chalk on the rail in line with the centers of the cue ball, the phantom cue ball and the aim point circle. Align the cue stick through the perpendicular center of the cue ball and the chalk on the rail.

Strike the cue ball maintaining this alignment of the cue stick. Strike the cue ball with sufficient speed to meet the objective. If everything has been performed according to instruction then you should properly execute the shot pattern. Try the same shot over and over again until you memorize the shot pattern. Try different shot patterns. Place the shot pattern in different places on the table to develop your expertise in completing any shot pattern that develops in the game.

B. Numerous bank shot diagrams will be illustrated. Each diagram will show the limitations of the bank shot when played according to the cue ball hit point. Other diagrams can be generated by using a different cue ball hit point. One problem in generating profuse diagrams with various cue ball hit points is the ability to recall the shot patterns from memory. Another problem is that individual players do not always strike the cue ball the same way so that the other diagrams generated may need individual revision.

The bank shot diagrams may be photocopied and mounted on card stock for durability and ready reference when playing.

On the charts the line is drawn on the center of the path of travel for the cue ball or object ball. So if the cue ball or object ball is between the lines then you must make an interpretation. If the cue ball or object ball is outside the limits of the shot pattern then there must be a special consideration to making the shot or the shot may not be possible to be made. This is an individual players judgement based upon the ball positions.

One last point is the use of a sighting device on the rail. This can be a piece of chalk or a piece of plastic or something else of your choosing. Sometimes another player will assist by placing his finger in position for sighting and sometimes the executing player may wet the rail cloth to make a mark

for sighting. Whatever the means
it would be helpful to have a
visible sighting device.

C. Every pocket billiard table is
rectangular in shape. It will
consist of two equal squares. Each
square is divided arbitrarily into
sixteen parts. So the table
consists of thirty two equal
squares. So there are eight
divisions along the long rail and
four divisions along the short
rail. Each division can be divided
again into tenths. This is then
called a diamond divider; ball
locater; or table divider. A few
common size dividers may be found
in this book. Photocopy the divider
and mount it on card stock for
durability. Place the divider in
position between the markings on
the table rail. You can place a
sighting device in position along
the divider. Sometimes the sighting
device should be placed on the
rubber cushion in line with the
correct designated marking on the
divider. See diagrams illustrating
"playing through the diamonds" for
an example on how to use the
diamond divider. The diamond

divider is also used in conjunction with the all purpose chart.

D. Another device is a hit point locater template. Place the template on the table and aim the arrow towards the desired objective. Make a depression in the center of the object ball circle and place an object ball on the depression. Place a sighting device on the rail in a line with the centers of the phantom cue ball and the cue ball. Aim through the center of the cue ball and the sighting device with the cue stick. Strike the cue ball with sufficient force to complete the shot.

E. A billiard protractor can be photocopied on transparency and cut out. Use the billiard protractor in conjunction with the all purpose chart and the cut shot templates shadow markings. The objective is to determine the amount of ball cover for aiming purposes on any given shot pattern.

F. An all purpose chart can be used in conjunction with the angle finder and the "playing through the

diamonds" diagrams. The pool table
chart can also be used as a ball
locater and kick shot indicator.

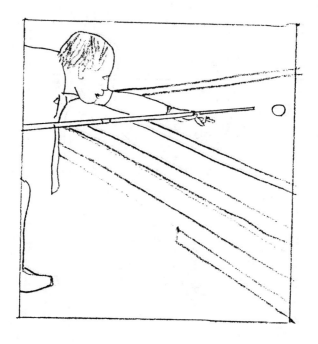

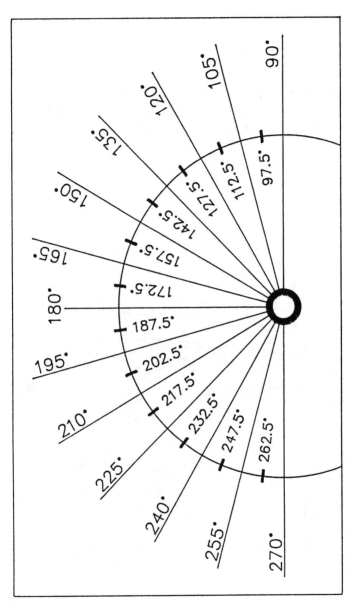

Billiard Protractor

170

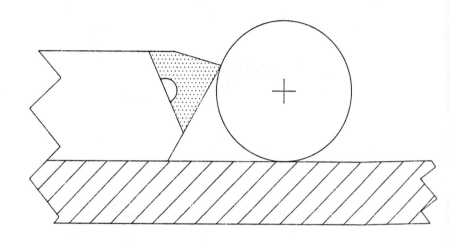

ILLUSTRATION

OF BALL HIT

POINT ON RAIL

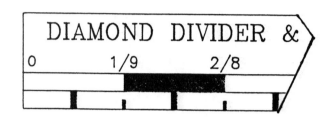

DIAMOND DIVIDER &

0   1/9   2/8

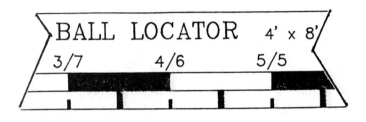

BALL LOCATOR   4' × 8'

3/7   4/6   5/5

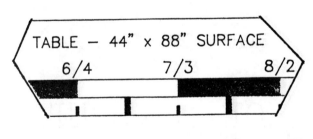

TABLE — 44" × 88" SURFACE

6/4   7/3   8/2

©1989 CHRIS RAFTIS

9/1   0

172

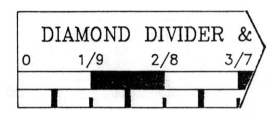

DIAMOND DIVIDER &

| 0 | 1/9 | 2/8 | 3/7 |

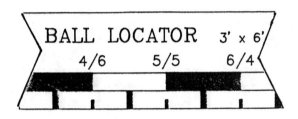

BALL LOCATOR 3' x 6'

| 4/6 | 5/5 | 6/4 |

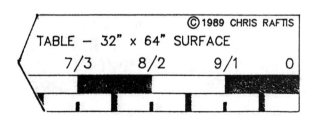

TABLE — 32" x 64" SURFACE

| 7/3 | 8/2 | 9/1 | 0 |

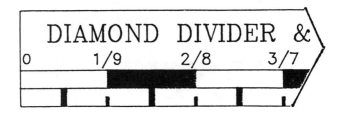

DIAMOND DIVIDER &

0   1/9   2/8   3/7

BALL LOCATOR   3 1/2'

4/6   5/5   6/4

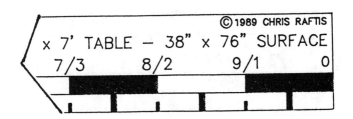

© 1989 CHRIS RAFTIS

x 7' TABLE — 38" x 76" SURFACE

7/3   8/2   9/1   0

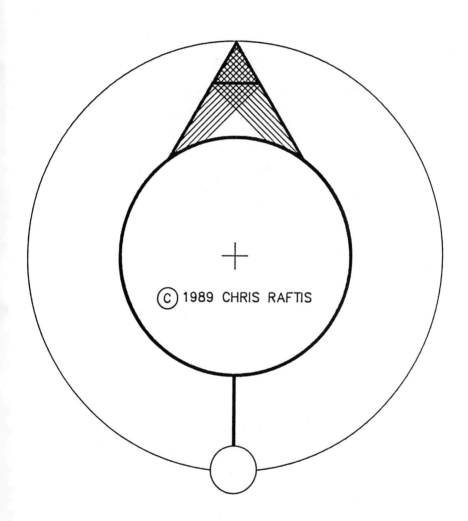

© 1989 CHRIS RAFTIS

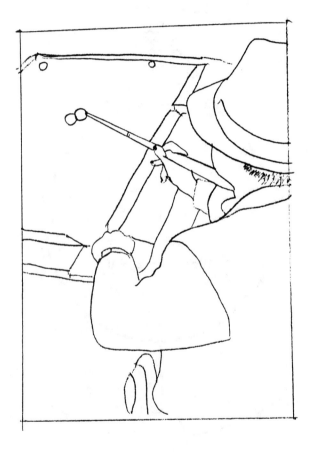

The Author

1930 Born in Indianapolis, Indiana, USA

1944 Introduced to pocket billiards in Mitchell, Indiana

1945 Learned the games of pocket billiards, especially snooker

1946 Managed a six table pocket billiards room

1951 Defeated Jake Ankrom-a well known local three cushion billiardist in Detroit, Michigan-state & national champion

1951 Defeated Jean La Rue, acclaimed worlds' one armed champion at snooker in Detroit, Michigan

1953 Established three pocket billiard centers in Kyoto, Japan

1962 Defeated oldest Gratzer brother at snooker in Bedford, Indiana-National Boys Club champion

1963 Defeated Eddy Taylor, known as the Knoxville Bear, at nine ball just after he won the Worlds Championship in Johnson City, Illinois. We played "jacked up" in Dayton, Ohio and I won eleven games to six.

1966 Produced newspaper syndication series entitled "CUE TIPS" a two column six inch insert with a fifty four page practice shot booklet

1988 Won the national eight ball championship held in San Antonio, Texas by the National VA Wheelchair Games, eight games to nothing in division four novice.

1988 Wrote and published a 127 page booklet on How to play at pool entitled "CUE TIPS"

1988 Started free clinics for the handicapped-Detroit,MI

1989 Won the division four masters classification in a national eight ball tournament in Long Beach, California conducted by the National VA Wheelchair Games-eight games to nothing

1990 Compiled and published home
study guides on bank, kick and cut
shots.

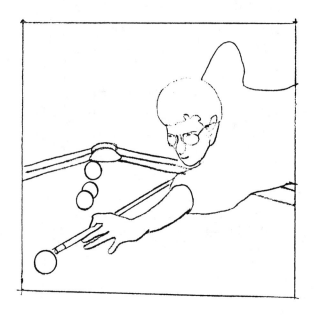

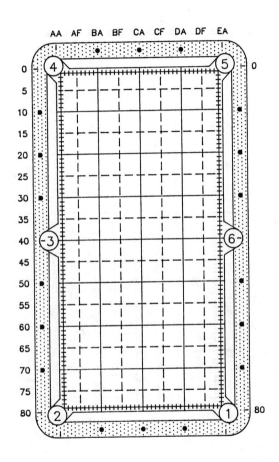

ALL PURPOSE CHART

LISTING OF DIAGRAMS AND SKETCHES

Fig.01	Richard Clancy playing at golf	4
Fig.02	Dominic Zito playing 9 ball	66
Fig.03	The angle of deviation = angle of adjustment	59
Fig.04	The extended table theory 114	115
Fig.05	Angle of incidence=angle of reflection	74
Fig.06	Angle of incidence=angle of reflection	73
Fig.07	Angle of incidence=angle of reflection	72
Fig.08	Angle of incidence=angle of reflection	71
Fig.09	Angle of incidence=angle of reflection	70
Fig.10	Angle of incidence=angle of reflection	67
Fig.11	Angle of incidence=angle of reflection	75
Fig.12	Cut shot chart no. one	60
Fig.13	Cut shot chart no. two	61
Fig.14	Cut shot chart no. three	62
Fig.15	Cut shot chart no. four	63
Fig.16	Cut shot chart no. five	64
Fig.17	Cut shot chart no. six	65
Fig.18	Cut shot template 90 deg.	39
Fig.19	Cut shot template 105 deg.	43
Fig.20	Cut shot template 120 deg.	37
Fig.21	Cut shot template 135 deg.	40
Fig.22	Cut shot template 150 deg.	42

181

Fig.23 Cut shot template 165 deg.   45
Fig.24 Cut shot template 195 deg.   41
Fig.25 Cut shot template 210 deg.   46
Fig.26 Cut shot template 225 deg.   36
Fig.27 Cut shot template 240 deg.   35
Fig.28 Cut shot template 255 deg.   44
Fig.29 Cut shot template 270 deg.   38
Fig.30 Cut shot template 97.5 deg.   50
Fig.31 Cut shot template 112.5 deg.   56
Fig.32 Cut shot template 127.5 deg.   49
Fig.33 Cut shot template 142.5 deg.   55
Fig.34 Cut shot template 157.5 deg.   57
Fig.35 Cut shot template 172.5 deg.   51
Fig.36 Cut shot template 187.5 deg.   47
Fig.37 Cut shot template 202.5 deg.   58
Fig.38 Cut shot template 217.5 deg.   52
Fig.39 Cut shot template 232.5 deg.   54
Fig.40 Cut shot template 247.5 deg.   53
Fig.41 Cut shot template 262.5 deg.   48
Fig.42 Ball hit point on rail   171
Fig.43 Kick shot ref. 1 of 4   116
Fig.44 Kick shot ref. 2 of 4   117
Fig.45 Kick shot ref. 3 of 4   118
Fig.46 Kick shot ref. 4 of 4   119
Fig.47 Kick shot ref. 1 of 5   124
Fig.48 Kick shot ref. 2 of 5   125
Fig.49 Kick shot ref. 3 of 5   126
Fig.50 Kick shot ref. 4 of 5   127
Fig.51 Kick shot ref. 5 of 5   128
Fig.52 Kick shot ref. 1 of 4   120
Fig.53 Kick shot ref. 2 of 4   121
Fig.54 Kick shot ref. 3 of 4   122

Fig.55 Kick shot ref. 4 of 4   123
Fig.56 How to use protractor   186
Fig.57 Jeff Hoeksema's jump shot 130&131
Fig.58 Bank shot chart   87
Fig.59 Bank shot chart   88
Fig.60 Bank shot chart   89
Fig.61 Bank shot chart   90
Fig.62 Bank shot chart   91
Fig.63 Bank shot chart   92
Fig.64 Bank shot chart   93
Fig.65 Bank shot chart   94
Fig.66 Bank shot chart   95
Fig.67 Bank shot chart   96
Fig.68 Bank shot chart   97
Fig.69 Bank shot chart   98
Fig.70 Bank shot chart   99
Fig.71 Bank shot chart   100
Fig.72 Bank shot chart   101
Fig.73 Kick shot   106
Fig.74 Kick shot   105
Fig.75 Kick shot   104
Fig.76 Kick shot   103
Fig.77 Kick shot   107
Fig.78 Kick shot   108
Fig.79 Kick shot   110
Fig.80 Draw and kick shot   109
Fig.81 Kick shot   111
Fig.82 Bank shot one rail corner   84
Fig.83 Bank shot two rails side   85
Fig.84 Umbrella shot   112
Fig.85 Playing thru the diamonds   69
Fig.86 Playing thru the diamonds   68

Fig.87 Ball speed chart   34
Fig.88 All purpose chart   180
Fig.89 Diamond divider   172
Fig.90 Diamond divider   173
Fig.91 Diamond divider   174
Fig.92 Bank shot one rail side   77
Fig.93 Bank shot one rail corner   76
Fig.94 Bank shot one rail side   83
Fig.95 Bank shot one rail corner   82
Fig.96 Bank shot two rails side   80
Fig.97 Bank shot two rails corner   78
Fig.98 Bank shot two rails corner   79
Fig.99 Bank shot five rails corner   81
Fig.100 Hit point locater template   175
Fig.101 Billiard protractor   170
Fig.102 Sketch of author,C.Raftis   176

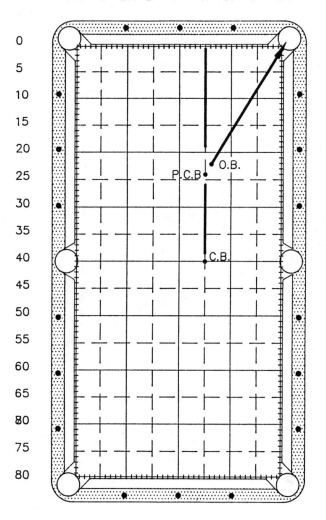

AA AF BA BF CA CF DA DF EA

0
5
10
15
20
25
30
35
40
45
50
55
60
65
80
75
80

P.C.B
O.B.
C.B.

HOW TO USE
PROTRACTOR

STEP FOUR
150°CUT